AA POCKET GUIDE

F ES

Written by Gerry Crawshaw
Verified by Robin Gauldie
Peace and Quiet section
by Paul Sterry

First published 1992 as *Essential Rhodes*
Reprinted 1993
Revised second edition 1994
Reprinted 1995 (twice)
Revised third edition 1997
Reprinted Nov 1998
Reprinted Oct and Nov 1999
Reprinted as *Pocket Guide Rhodes* 2000

Published by AA Publishing, a trading name of Automobile Association Developments Limited, whose registered office is Norfolk House, Priestley Road, Basingstoke, Hampshire, RG24 9NY.
Registered number 1878835.

Distributed in the United Kingdom by AA Publishing, Norfolk House, Priestley Road, Basingstoke, Hampshire, RG24 9NY.

A CIP catalogue record for this book is available from the British Library.

ISBN 0 7495 2479 0

Colour separation: BTB Colour Reproduction Ltd., Whitchurch, Hampshire.

Printed by: Printers S.R.L., Trento Italy.

Front cover picture: *Temple of Apollo (AA Photo Library – S L Day)*

Author's Acknowledgements
The author is indebted to Hogg Robinson Travel for permission to make use of regularly updated information on holiday resorts and hotels in Rhodes.

Contents

Country Distinguishing Signs

On some maps, international distinguishing signs have been used to identify those countries which surround Rhodes.
Thus:

(TR) = Turkey

This book employs a simple rating system to help choose which places to visit:

✓ 'top ten'

◆◆◆ do not miss
◆◆ see if you can
◆ worth seeing if you have time

INTRODUCTION

The Greek island of Rhodes or Ródos, to give it its Greek name, has practically everything anyone could possibly expect from a holiday island... delightful beaches nestling in craggy bays or stretching beyond eyesight; sun-bleached villages rising up the side of hills and mountains; and the spirit of an island steeped in centuries of history and mythology.

When Helios, the sun god, blessed it with light and warmth and favoured it with a delightful climate and lush vegetation, he may not have thought that Rhodes would one day become the most visited of the Dodecanese islands. And though resorts have mushroomed along the coastline, offering varied facilities and entertainment to satisfy most visitors' needs, the people of Rhodes are still likely to greet you with genuine warmth and hospitality and to take great pride in sharing with you their jewel in the Aegean Sea.

The largest of the Dodecanese islands, Rhodes is in the Aegean Sea, on the southeastern edge

Bronzes of a stag and doe, ancient emblems of Rhodes, stand guard over the mouth of Mandraki Harbour

of the Dodecanese, facing Turkey 10 miles (16km) away. Smaller than Crete but larger than Corfu, it is approximately diamond shaped, being about 40 miles (65km) long and 25 miles (40km) wide, and enjoys a mild climate and long, sun-drenched summer days.

Thanks to its situation at the crossroads of three continents, the island has known many masters. Romans, Crusaders, Arabs, Turks and Italians have all left their mark, and today's visitors can marvel at the ruins of ancient temples, admire elaborate mosques, wander narrow streets flanked by medieval inns, soak up the centuries-old atmosphere of the island's enchanting towns and villages, or venture inland to enjoy the rugged, olive-clad hillsides sheltering scented pine forests.

Rhodes is so different from most Greek isles that even Greeks tend to describe it as 'foreign'. Side by side you will find sophistication and simple Greek life, luxury hotels and little tavernas, smart entertainment and simple pleasures, international cuisine and simple Greek fare.

There are good beaches all around the coast,

Named after an English admiral, Monte Smith was once a suburb of ancient Rhodes, until the town shrank and nature reclaimed the hill

some with watersports, bars, smart restaurants and entertainment; others simple and almost deserted. And though midsummer temperatures can reach 85°F (30°C) and above, west winds soften the heat on many beaches.

Rhodes Town, the island's capital, is a remarkable and attractive blend of a lively harbour, a walled, fortified medieval town and a cosmopolitan, modern town.

Most visitors to the east coast of Rhodes understandably opt for Líndos, built on the ruins of an ancient Doric town of the same name. Despite being overrun by tourists in the high season, and commercialised to a degree many people consider unacceptable, there can be no denying that it is still a delightful, magical place… a little town of whitewashed houses built on the sides of a steep, rocky hill, crowned by an awe-inspiring castle built by the Knights of St John of Jerusalem.

There are many other delights on the east coast of Rhodes in addition to Líndos. The former spa resort of Thérmes Kalithéa is built round a colourful, pine-covered bay; Faliráki is a lively, cosmopolitan holiday resort with an excellent beach; Afántou is an ancient village with a golf course and an interesting church; and Tsampíka has a lovely, sandy shoreline as well as a mountain topped with a monastery dedicated to the Virgin Mary. The village of Archángelos is noteworthy for its traditional architecture, ceramics and carpet workshops, while Charáki, a former fishing village that is now a fast-developing holiday resort, lies on a lovely stretch of coast that contains the impressive ruins of Feráklos castle.

Popular holiday resorts, important archaeological sites and picturesque villages are to be found on the northwest coast of the island too, beginning with Rhodes Town itself and embracing the resorts of Triánta, on the doorstep of the impressive ancient city of Ialyssós, with its magnificent acropolis; the blossoming resort of Kremastí; and, slightly inland, the unusual Valley of the Petaloudhes (Butterflies), where from June to early September many thousands of butterflies (or, more correctly, moths) take refuge.

Then there is ancient Kameíros, the island's third

most important commercial city in ancient times; the delightful fishing village of Kameíros Skála; and fascinating Monólithos, built on the pine-covered slopes of Mount Attávyros, with a 15th-century castle on the cliffs.

Rhodes also has much to offer the visitor prepared to venture inland, with delightful, traditional villages little touched by tourism, and areas of great scenic beauty such as Profítis Ilías, with its panoramic sea views. But there is more to Rhodes than well-situated holiday resorts, historic sites and lovely landscapes. Modern hotels offer every comfort, and shopping is a pleasure. There is plenty for the active visitor too, with tennis, watersports, lovely walks and a well-designed golf course – to say nothing of cycling, a popular form of transport here. As for restaurants, tavernas, bars and discothèques, these abound in the major coastal resorts, and in Rhodes Town itself, with a sufficiently wide choice to cater for most tastes and pockets. And Rhodes' geographical position also provides for some interesting visits to other nearby islands; excursions to Sými are particularly popular with those choosing Rhodes as a holiday base.

Some resort areas on Rhodes have been allowed to grow excessively and haphazardly, prompted by a tourism boom which has now been reversed. Greece is no longer the cheapest destination in Europe, and Greek tourism authorities have called for higher quality services and facilities in every aspect of tourism. On Rhodes, as on other islands, these efforts have been hindered by niggardly international tour operators who are unwilling to pay Greek hoteliers enough to allow them to reinvest and improve their hotels. However, Rhodes is in the forefront of the campaign to offer visitors ever-better value for money. Local hoteliers and municipalities have realised that to compete in today's market they need to polish every facet of their island gem. As a result, beaches at resorts around the island are kept immaculately clean, and the houseproud Rhodians keep the streets and sights of their lovely island equally spotless and litter-free.

BACKGROUND

According to mythology, Rhodes was singled out for favour by the sun god Helios who, having been overlooked when Zeus distributed the lands of the world among the gods, discovered the island and made it his own, together with the beautiful nymph Rhodos, daughter of the sea god Poseidon, whom he took for his wife.

Ancient Rhodes grew rich on sea trade and, according to legend, the favour of the sun god

Beginnings

The first human inhabitants of the island are thought to have been a rugged, primitive people from Asia Minor who possessed great skills in the arts. On the basis of discoveries made in a cave in southern Rhodes, experts believe they settled there as early as the Stone Age, though it is thought they were subsequently overrun by waves of invaders during the Bronze Age – Carians from Anatolia, Phoenicians from present-day Lebanon, and Minoans from Crete.
The most significant early invaders, however, were the Achaeans from the Peloponnese who,

The Colossus of Rhodes, one of the seven wonders of the ancient world, stood more than 100 feet (30m) high. It is usually shown straddling the harbour, but archaeologists now believe it stood inland

by 1500 BC, had colonised the island. These were, in turn, replaced by Dorians who swept through Greece in about 1100 BC. On Rhodes they built shrines for moon worship at Ialyssós, Líndos and Kameíros, and also united with the island of Kos and the cities of Knidos and Halicarnassus in Asia Minor to form a federal league, the Dorian hexapolis.

Seafarers
For centuries the inhabitants of Rhodes, especially the men of Líndos, were great sailors. Trading took them to Asia, Greece and the western Mediterranean. Rhodian colonies were founded in the west – in Sicily, Spain and France.

Classical Period

In 491 BC Rhodes fought off the first attempt by Persian forces to take the island. Datis, who led the Persian attack, laid siege to Lindos but

withdrew his forces on learning that the goddess Athena had performed a miracle and supplied the water that the local population so desperately needed. The island was forced to become a Persian ally in the years that followed, however, and when Xerxes invaded the Greek mainland in 480 BC, 40 of the ships which fought on the Persian side at Salamis were Rhodian. The Greek victory in this great sea battle saw Rhodes enter a period of subjugation to Athens, and at the end of the Persian wars the three cities on Rhodes (Ialyssós, Líndos and Kameíros) became members of the 1st Athenian Confederacy (478–7 BC). Then, towards the end of the 5th century BC, the Rhodians decided to found a new city on the northern tip of the island – a model, walled city designed by the leading town planner of the day and sited to satisfy defence and trade needs, with five new harbours.

The new city soon became the major trading power in the eastern Mediterranean and one of the great cultural centres of the Hellenistic and Roman worlds. As it increased in importance, the three older cities suffered a gradual decline. The city of Rhodes' pre-eminence lasted for several centuries. In the 3rd century BC, for example, its population is estimated to have been between 60,000 and 80,000, two or three times larger than that of today. And the contribution of the island to the arts, trade and law of the time was significant.

In the troubled period that followed the death of Alexander the Great, however, Rhodes was attacked in 305–4 BC by a huge force led by Demetrios Poliorkites (son of one of Alexander's generals and himself a brilliant commander). Demetrios was the foremost military engineer of his time, and when he came to Rhodes he was already known as 'The Besieger', a title gained following his success against a city in Cyprus. The siege of Rhodes, however – which lasted a year – failed to justify his reputation, with the city emerging intact largely thanks to its strong defence walls. The Rhodians sold the siege machines left behind by Demetrios and used the huge revenue from the sale to erect a tribute to their god Helios – the Colossus of Rhodes. The mighty statue was to collapse during an earthquake in 226 BC.

In 164 BC Rhodes entered into an ill-fated alliance with Rome which culminated in an attack by Cassius in 42 BC. Cassius sacked the island, stripped it of many thousand works of art which he sent to Rome, confiscated public and private money, allowed the citizens to be butchered, and finally set fire to what was left.

Medieval Rhodes

Christianity took root in Rhodes during the 1st century AD, aided by St Paul, who visited the island on his way to Syria, about 20 years after the Crucifixion. But this did not lead to a period of peace or stability, and by the end of the 4th century AD, Rhodes had exchanged the rule of Rome for that of Byzantium. But this change did not lead to happier times either. Indeed, in the ensuing centuries the island was attacked by numerous invaders... Goths in the 5th century, Arabs in the 7th and 9th centuries, and then Saracens, Venetians, Franks and Genoese. Rhodes' ties with western Europe were strengthened in 1097 with the appearance of the Crusaders on their way to the Holy Land. In 1191, King Richard the Lionheart of England and King Philip Augustus of France landed in Rhodes to recruit mercenaries. Byzantium was captured by the Crusaders 13 years later, and the tide of battle turned. By 1291 the Christian army was forced off the beaches at Acre, today part of Israel.

Knights of St John

Among the retreating soldiers were the Knights of the Order of St John of Jerusalem – or Knights Hospitallers as they are sometimes referred to in order to distinguish them from the Knights Templars, members of the Order of the Poor Knights of Christ.

The Knights of St John originated in the 11th century at the Hospital of St John of Jerusalem, a Benedictine hospital for pilgrims. The Order was founded to care for the poor and sick, train doctors, protect pilgrims, and make war on the infidel. Their first patron was St John the Almsgiver, a 6th-century Cypriot bishop, and in 1113 the Order and its possessions were taken under the protection of Pope Paschal II in gratitude for the services which the hospital had provided during the Crusades.

The Knights of St John took an active part in the Crusades but, following the fall of the last Christian stronghold in Palestine, they were driven out of Palestine not only by the forces of Saladin but through bitter rivalry with the powerful Knights Templars.

The Knights of St John emigrated to Cyprus in 1291, but in 1309 decided to transfer to Rhodes, believing this to be a better base. However, the Greek pirates who had taken over the island in 1248 refused to allow the Knights to settle there. Undeterred, they decided to buy it, and a bill of sale was drawn up and witnessed.

The Knights nevertheless had to fight for their rights, defeating – with the aid of the Genoans – the garrison placed on the island by the Byzantine emperor. Once settled on Rhodes, the Knights established a hospital, continued to improve the island's defences, and for two centuries succeeded in holding out against marauding Turkish corsairs, building up a powerful fleet of war galleys, and becoming in the process excellent seamen.

Privileged Knights

Members of the Order of St John came from all the European Catholic countries, and were divided into classes based on the degree of nobility of their origins and the services they offered as soldiers, nurses or clerics. The organisation was based on the country of origin, and they were divided into seven Tongues (ie languages) or national groups: Provence, Auvergne, France, Italy, Germany, England and Spain (which was later divided into Aragon and Castille, increasing the number of Tongues to eight). United by vows of obedience and chastity, they were divided into five groups: Military Knights, Conventual Chaplains, Serving Brothers, Magistral Knights and Knights of Grace. It was the Military Knights who gave the Order its distinctive characteristics and from whom the Grand Masters were chosen. Before being admitted to the Order they were required to prove noble birth on both sides of their families for at least four generations, and so honourable was a career in this aristocratic foreign legion considered that it became the practice to put younger sons' names down at birth.

As the Knights' wealth and power increased, the Turks launched a large-scale attack in 1479, but were driven back. The following year, however, Sultan Souleïmán I decided to launch another attack. His force of 70,000 men aboard 200 ships landed near Ialyssós on 24 June, and three months later laid siege to Rhodes with the sultan in command. In four and a half months Souleïmán lost 50,000 men trying to penetrate the fortified city, one attack resulting in the death of 9,000 Turks and half the Knights. The surviving Knights immediately set about rebuilding and improving the defences, and within a short time Rhodes became the strongest fortress in the west. But the Turks were undeterred, and 42 years later launched an even more massive attack. Although heavily outnumbered, the Knights put up a spirited defence, so much so that the Turks were on the verge of giving up, only to have second thoughts when a traitor revealed that victory was in their grasp. The invaders launched a final assault, and succeeded in breaching the walls.

As a result, after 145 days of siege the 180 surviving Knights, together with 4,000 Catholic Rhodians, were allowed to depart on 1 January 1523. They returned to Cyprus, and nine years later were given the sovereignty of Malta by the Emperor Charles V, after which they were generally known as the Knights of Malta. They remained in control of Malta until 1798 when they were deposed by Napoleon and took refuge in Russia.

The Order was reconstituted in 1879 by the papacy as a charitable organisation for the care of the sick and wounded, the Order's emblem being a white Maltese cross on a black background.

Turkish and Italian Occupation

For nearly four centuries, until 1912, Rhodes remained a minor Turkish possession. Reminders of the Turks' occupation can be seen in the walled town, with its mosques and minarets, fountains, carvings and courtyards. The Italians came to Rhodes in 1912, and occupied the island until 1943. At first they were regarded as liberators but their time was one of great hardship and oppression for the island – much more so than under the Turks – yet the Italians did leave behind them good roads, well-landscaped gardens, a number of public buildings and a great many private villas. During their occupation they also rebuilt the Palace of the Grand Masters (they regarded themselves as heirs of the Knights of St John) and undertook a considerable amount of restoration on classical sites.

Anáktoro ton Arkhónton has been in turn the Knights' headquarters, a Turkish prison and an Italian palace

Recent Times

After the fall of Mussolini's government in 1943, Rhodes was occupied by German troops until 1945 when Greek and British forces recaptured the island. Following a period of United Nations trusteeship, it was reunited with Greece in 1947, and is now the administrative capital for the islands which make up the Dodecanese – notably Astypálaia, Chálki, Kárpathos, Kásos, Tílos, Nísyros, Kálymnos, Léros, Pátmos, Ródos, Sými, Kos, Psérimos and Leipsoí.

The population of Rhodes today is about 67,000 with the biggest concentration in Rhodes Town.

The enormous development of tourism has transformed Rhodes' economy in recent years, although much of the population is still engaged in agriculture. The cultivable area of the island forms about 18 per cent of the whole, the main products being wine, oil, tobacco, garden produce and cereals. Cattle raising is also important, since 34 per cent of the terrain is pastureland. The forests are also a source of revenue, covering 37 per cent of the territory, and are home to a type of deer known as *platoni* – a rare animal that is one of Rhodes' emblems, and a protected species.

Plateía Ippokratous is at the heart of the charming Old Town

RHODES TOWN (RÓDOS)

Rhodes Town is situated at the northern tip of the island, and is one of the busiest and liveliest resorts in the whole of Greece, attracting visitors from all over Europe. It is a captivating town. The powerful impression given by the great walls and dominant Palace of the Grand Masters (Anáktoro ton Arkhónton), is tempered by elegant minarets and colonnades and gardens lush with greenery and bright with bougainvillea and hibiscus. The town comprises two quite separate but complementary sections – the ancient, medieval walled city known as the Old Town; and the modern city known, not surprisingly, as the New Town. Both sections are well worth visiting.

The Old Town, with its impressive, 15th-century buildings, cobbled streets and alleys ornamented with arches and vaults, its impressive museums, countless shops, scores of atmospheric bars, tavernas and restaurants, and traditional coffee shops, is understandably the jewel in the crown. Here you will find such riches as the unique Street of the Knights, arguably the most splendid medieval street in the world, although heavily restored in recent years; the fascinating Museum of Rhodes (Mouseío Archaiologikó), housed in a 15th-century building which originally served as the hospital of the Knights of St John; the Museum of Decorative Arts (Mouseío tis Kosmikís Téchnis), with its interesting display of folk art; and the equally interesting Municipal Art Gallery (Astikí Pinakothíki), with its exhibition of modern art by Greek painters. Here, too, you will find the impressive Palace of the Grand Masters, built on the site of an

RHODES TOWN

ancient temple dedicated to Rhodes' patron deity, the sun god Helios, and now a museum; the Turkish baths, still in use; and numerous 16th-century mosques built by Souleïmán the Magnificent. Whereas the Old Town is a treasure-trove of towers, battlements, mosques and fine medieval buildings and streets, the New Town is where the beaches lie and where hotels, shops, restaurants, café-bars and discothèques are packed together to create a lively, cosmopolitan ambience. The New Town also contains much to interest the sightseer, including bustling Mandraki Harbour, where floating gin-palaces rub sterns with more traditional boats; the Néa Agorá (New Market), has an inner courtyard alive with stalls, a fish market, and shops, cafés and bars.

Other impressive buildings on or near the harbour are the Archbishop's Palace (Paláti Arkhiepískopou), Church of the Annunciation (Eklissía Evangelismós), Town Hall (Dimarcheío), and National Theatre (Ethnikó Théatro), while also of particular interest in the New Town are the Mosque (Tzamí) of Mourad Reïs, with its graceful minaret, and the Aquarium (Enydríon). Rhodes Town has two beaches, both extremely crowded in the high season, and consisting mainly of coarse sand. That on the east side of town is sandier than that on the west, which has a busy main road running behind it. Children need to be supervised, since the sea bed shelves steeply.

RÓDOS
0
100
200
300 m
Limáni Mandrákiou
Emporikó Limáni
Limáni Akandías
Tzamí tou Mourad Reïs
Sýllogos Thalamigón
Ethnikó Théatro
Nomarcheío
Ochyró tou Agíou Nikoláou
Dimarcheío
Ekklisía Evangelismoú
Anemómyli
EOT
Néa Agorá
'Íchos kai Fos'
Astikí Pinakothíki
Paláti Ippotón
Mouseío tis Kosmikís Téchnis
Pand Provence
Pand Auvergne
Italikó Pand
Anglikó Pand
Telonío
Ispanikó Pandocheío
Gallikó Pand
Mouseío Archaiologikó
Emporodikeío
Tzamí Suleïman
Tourkikí Vivliothíki
Tzamí Sultan Mustafá
Tzamí tou Aga
Paláti Archiepískopou
Bánio
Théatro
Tzamí Retset Pascha
Ágios Fanoúrios (Pial-el-Din)
Stádio
PAPANIKOLAOU
PL KOUNDOURIÓTOU
POLYTECHNEÍO
AMERIKIS
IERÓU LÓCHOU
IROÓN
PL AKADIMÍAS
25 MARTÍOU
ELEFTHERÍAS
S VENIZÉLOU
LAMPRAKI
MAKARIOU
PLASTIRA
GALLIAS
PL RIMINÍ
ALEX PAPAGOU
DIMOKRATÍAS
PÝLI AMBOUAZ
PÝLI ELEFTHERÍAS
PÝLI AGÍOU PAVLOU
PL SÝMIS
PÝLI NAVARCHÍOU
PL ARGYROKÁSTROU
PL KLEOVOÚLOU
IPPOTÓN
PL MOUSEÍO
ORFÉOS
ERMOÚ
PÝLI AGÍA AIKATERÍNIS
PÝLI MILÓN
AKTÍ SACHTOURI
SOKRATOUS
PL IPPOKRÁTOUS
PL ARIÓNOS
PL ATHÍNAS
AG FANOURÍOU
PL MARTYRÓN EVRAÍON
ALHADEF
PÝLI KARETOU
IPPODAMOU
PYTHAGORA
PERIKLÉOUS
OMÍROU
KOMNINÓN
PÝLI AGÍOU ATHANASSÍOU
PÝLI AGÍOU IOÁNNOU
VYRONOS
FILÉLLINON
KANADÁ
ÁGIOS LAVRAS
ÁGIOS ANARGYRON
KONSTANTÍNOU
KODRICTONOS
XANTHOU
E BEVIN
KO

WHAT TO SEE

◆◆◆
ANÁKTORO TON ARKHÓNTON (PALACE OF THE GRAND MASTERS) ✓

Platia Kleovoulou, Old Town
Dominating the northeast sector of the city's fortifications, this imposing, turreted building – now a museum – is a reconstruction of a palace built by Helion de Villeneuve on the site of an ancient temple to the sun god Helios. After serving as the Knight's palace, it was turned into a prison by the Turks, who also used it for stabling their horses. Following centuries of neglect it was destroyed by an ammunition explosion in the palace vaults in 1856. The explosion – thought to have been set off by lightning – killed an estimated 800 people. The great door of the palace between the two round towers is one of the parts preserved from the original building. Beyond it is a large, covered area, with the entrance to the main building on the left, and straight ahead an interior courtyard surrounded by arches containing a variety of

Paláti Ippotón's great door

Italian Villa
The Palace was rebuilt in questionable taste, by the Italians as a summer home for Mussolini and Victor Emmanuel III. Because of its intended use, it was made even grander than the original. The exterior you see today is a reasonable approximation of the 14th-century original, and was completed by the Italians just before the outbreak of World War II. Inside, they installed central heating, concealed lifts, translucent alabaster windows, Roman statuary and mosaics. But the interior was scarcely completed when the Italian occupation came to an end.

statues. A small chapel contains Roman and Christian objects. Inside, a marble staircase leads to rooms paved with mosaics and furnished with statues, Italian furniture, wall carpets and Chinese vases. Of the palace's 200 rooms – 14 of which are open to the public – the most impressive are the throne and ceremonial rooms. The fine Roman and early Christian mosaics are not part of the original furnishing, but were removed from the nearby island of Kos by the Italians. The most interesting is a 1st-century AD representation of the nine Muses covering the floor of an entire room. The long passages are furnished with numerous choir stalls.
Excellent views of the town and surroundings can be enjoyed from the palace windows and also from its garden.
Open: daily, 08.30–15.00hrs.
Closed: Mondays.

◆◆◆
MOUSEÍO ARCHAIOLOGIKÓ (MUSEUM OF RHODES) ✓

Platia Mouseío, Old Town
The most important antique objects discovered in Rhodes and the other islands making up the Dodecanese are displayed in the impressive medieval building that was once the Hospital of the Knights of St John of Jerusalem. Construction of the building began in 1440 when the Knights' original hospital became too small, and it was completed in 1489, in Gothic style. In common with most of the Street of the Knights (see page 25), the building was restored in the early 1900s, and has been a museum since 1916.
With an arcaded courtyard and a wide flight of steps leading to a gallery which runs round three sides of the square, almost the whole of the building's east side is occupied by the **Infirmary Hall**, widely considered one of the most impressive medieval rooms in Europe. Nearly 100 yards (90m) long, it has a vaulted roof supported by arches springing from the seven pillars which divide the hall lengthwise. In this chamber there was room for 32 canopied beds for sick or wounded Knights, attended night and day by surgeons and orderlies, the care of the sick being the original reason for the Order's foundation.
At the south end of the hall a door leads into a room which served as the hospital refectory, and this in turn leads into three rooms which house the museum's collection of statuary.

The rooms on the south side of the museum display finds from the excavations of cemeteries in the area of ancient Ialyssós – mostly vases from the 9th to the 5th centuries BC. In the centre of the east side is the entrance to the infirmary, containing

Coats of arms of the Knights on display in the Mouseío Archaiologikó

gravestones from the period of the Knights, and many coats of arms, while the refectory or dining room for hospital staff is used to display funerary stele (columns) from the Roman period. Of interest here is a beautifully executed and preserved funerary stele of two female figures – Timarista, on the right, and her daughter Krito – embracing in a final farewell. Of the museum's many exhibits, however, one of the most impressive is the tall figure of the **Aphrodite of Rhodes**, otherwise known as the 'Marine Venus', having been found in the sea by fishermen early this century. It is on display in what is known as the **Room of the Small Aphrodite**. Aphrodite is represented kneeling, either before or after bathing, in a posture suggesting she is either loosening or tying up her hair, and the artist has succeeded in showing off the female form to good advantage. Such statues adorned the houses of wealthy Rhodians around 100 BC, and were also used as ornaments in public gardens. The Aphrodite of Rhodes is an example of ancient rococo which flourished at the end of the Hellenistic period in Rhodes – an art that sought to titillate the senses and capture a fleeting moment. The same room also contains a series of small statues, the most impressive of which is that of Asklepios (god of healing) with a snake twined round his staff. From here you come out on to a delightful gallery planted with flowers and shrubs which looks down on a small courtyard with a 6th-century mosaic pavement brought from Kárpathos. On the north side of the gallery are two rooms with more exhibits of considerable interest. One, labelled 'Hekataion', shows three female figures standing on the backs of lions. This was discovered on the acropolis (Monte Smith). Look out also for the fine, headless statue of a nymph with her foot on a rock, which dates from the 1st century BC.

The museum's courtyard displays a medley of exhibits: a marble crouching lion, some 2,000 years old; piles of cannon balls from the time of the Turkish invasion; catapult shot; and a mosaic, dating from 650 BC, from Arkasa on the island of Kárpathos, between Rhodes and Crete.

Open: daily 08.30–15.00hrs. Closed Mondays.

◆
ASTIKÍ PINAKOTHÍKI (MUNICIPAL ART GALLERY)

Platia Sýmis, Old Town

A modern building in medieval style, this features exhibitions of modern art by Greek painters, and is located up a flight of stairs over the Ionian and Popular Bank. Of particular note are the works by Theophilos, an artist from the island of Mytilini (Lesbos), who specialised in the primitive style. An itinerant artist, Theophilos died in 1934. *Open*: daily 08.00–14.00hrs and also on Wednesdays 17.00–20.00hrs.

◆◆
AGIOS FANOÚRIOS

Omirou, Old Town

The original Byzantine church and its frescoes were taken over by the Turks who, at first, used the building as stables, destroying the lower wall paintings. Later it was converted into the Pial-el-Din Mosque, only for the Greeks to reclaim it and reconvert it to the Orthodox faith. The Italians restored the paintings towards the end of their occupation of Rhodes.

Byzantine frescoes grace Agios Fanoúrios's barrel vault

◆◆
BÁNIO (BATH HOUSE)
Platia Ariónos, Old Town
The fantastic Turkish baths on Platia Ariónos, in the southwest corner of the Old Town, is one of only a few public baths in Greece still in use. Constructed in 1765, the building was seriously damaged during World War II and subsequently rebuilt. The old marble floor remains, and the reconstruction was carried out sympathetically. Sexes are strictly segregated in the sauna.
Open: Monday to Friday 05.00–19.00hrs and slightly shorter hours on Wednesdays and Saturdays, when admission charges are cheaper.
Closed: Sundays.

◆
EMPORODIKEÍO (TRIBUNE OF COMMERCE)
Platia Ippokratous, Old Town
Completed in 1507, the building was the court-house of the Knights. The first floor is reached by wide, external stone steps and supported by columns which form a ground level arcade. The doorway, which is decorated with carved coats of arms, is worthy of a close look.

◆◆
ENYDRÍON (AQUARIUM)
Kalimnou Lerou, New Town
Located within a building bearing the grandiose name of Hydrobiological Institute, standing at the northern extremity of Rhodes Town, the Aquarium houses embalmed marine and other animals and large tanks full of fish and invertebrates such as starfish, octopus and sponges, and is said to be the only museum of its kind in Greece.
Open: daily 09.00–21.00hrs.

One of the weird exhibits at the Enydríon, Rhodes' aquarium museum

◆◆◆ IPPOTÓN (STREET OF THE KNIGHTS) ✓

Old Town

Leading due east from the Palace Square, the beautiful, if much restored, Street of the Knights is lined with inns which once housed the Knights of St John according to the language they spoke. Each of the Seven (later Eight) Tongues of the Order had its own residence, five of them located in the street. The **Inn of France** (Gallikó Pandocheío) is the best-preserved example, with an elaborate façade bearing an off-centre doorway decorated with seven coats of arms and crocodile gargoyles. The coats of arms belong to the Order of St John and to the two Grand Masters who built the inn – d'Amboise and d'Aubusson. The date above the pointed arch of the main entrance, 1492, is the year work on the building began. Visitors are welcome to inspect the building, which is still used occasionally as a recital hall and for exhibitions. Next to it is the **Inn of Spain** (Ispanikó Pandocheío), built in a style reflecting its Catalan influence. Near this once stood the Church of St John, the Knights' chief place of worship. It was blown up in the explosion of 1856 in the Palace of the Grand Masters. A replica of questionable authenticity was built by the Italians at Mandraki Harbour in 1925.

The **Inn of Italy** (Italikó Pandocheío) was restored during the period of the Italian occupation to resemble the original building. Over the sculpted doors is the emblem of Fabrizio del Caretto, a Grand Master who died in 1479, a year before the Turkish Sultan Souleïmán's assault.

The **Inn of Provence** (Pandocheío Provence) was a later addition to the street, dating from the early 16th century. It has a less ornate façade than its counterparts.

Nothing remains of the **Inn of Germany** except for a plane tree which marks the site where it once stood.

Halfway down the street is a shady garden visible beyond locked gates. Containing a lovely Turkish fountain, the garden has been the subject of recent restoration.

One of the oldest buildings in the street is the **French Chapel**, containing a niche for a statue of the Virgin and Child with Fleur-de-lis. Next door is the chaplain's residence, now housing the Italian vice-consulate.

The **Inn of England** (Anglikó Pandocheío) is situated not in Ippotón itself, but on Platia Mouseío, across from the Archaeological Museum, and was built in 1483. It was destroyed in 1851 by an earthquake, rebuilt in 1919 by the Italians and further restored by the British after World War II, following severe damage from shelling. Of particular interest is a room displaying the works of a leading modern goldsmith. The **Inn of Auvergne** (Pandocheío Auvergne) is also situated away from the Street of the Knights on Platia Sýmis. Today it houses state offices.

◆◆
JEWISH QUARTER
Old Town

The old Jewish quarter lies to the east of the Koskinou Gate (Pýli Koskinou). Its most prominent feature is the drum-shaped **fountain** in Plateía Martyrón Evraión (Square of the Martyrs), which is topped by three bronze sea horses and decorated with blue tiles, in turn decorated with shells and marine creatures. The square is dedicated to the Jews transported from Rhodes during World War II. A poignant plaque on the wall of the synagogue on nearby Odos Dosiadou records that 2,000 Rhodian Jews still resident when German troops took over the island in July 1943 were assembled in this square before being transported to concentration camps, only 50 surviving.
The square is also the location of the 15th-century **Archbishop's Palace**, a mish-mash of Gothic and Renaissance architecture. This housed the archbishop of the Greek Orthodox church prior to Souleïmán the Magnificent's invasion.

Mandraki harbour is for leisure boats, like these yachts; island ferries leave from the neighbouring Commercial Harbour.

◆◆◆
LIMÁNI MANDRÁKIOU (MANDRAKI HARBOUR) ✓

New Town
Guarded by two pillars supporting a bronze stag and doe, the harbour area is packed with strollers and sightseers who come here to enjoy the flavour and animation as well as the cafés and bars. This is where the Municipal Tourist Office (in Platia Rimini) and the Néa Agorá are located, and where the taxis and buses stop. The harbour also has a yacht marina, the local fishing boat fleet, excursion boats, and the smaller inter-island ferries.

Shops backing on to the Néa Agorá sell olives and nuts and duty-free drinks, while popular spots for sitting and watching the world go by are the cafés underneath the arches opposite the harbour. Other attractions for visitors are the trio of picturesque **windmills**, dating from the late 1400s, in which grain for the cargo ships was milled, and the 15th-century **fortress of St Nicholas** (Ochyró tou Agíou Nikoláou Fáros) which still guards the harbour, sporting a guiding lighthouse. It was built in 1464 with funds supplied by Philip the Good of Burgundy. In 1480, during the second of the Turkish sieges, the fort was greatly strengthened around the base and was later elaborated still more. Within its walls is a small church, dedicated to St Nicholas. At the northern end of the harbour the **Governor's House** (Nomarcheío), with its Venetian Gothic arches, is also popular with photographers. The name Mandraki, meaning sheepfold, reflects the earlier commercial function of the port.

Platoni *guarding the harbour entrance*

The Colossus of Rhodes
Mandraki Harbour is reputedly the location of one of the most famous statues of all time. A tribute to the sun god Helios, the statue was massive – more than 100 feet (30m) tall, and was cast in bronze by the sculptor Chares of Lindos. The work took him 12 years. A masterpiece of technical and artistic achievement, it was considered one of the Seven Wonders of the Ancient World. But it stood for little more than 60 years before being felled by an earthquake in 226 BC.
Modern scholars cast doubt on the traditional theory that the statue straddled the harbour, with its massive feet on either side allowing ships to pass between its legs.

◆◆◆
MONTE SMITH
about 1 mile (2km) west of Rhodes Town
This hill was the site of the ancient Hellenistic town of Rhodes. It makes a pleasant walk from the town in the evening.

Monte Smith
Originally known as Agios Stephanos, this hill has been known as Monte Smith since the time of the Napoleonic wars, when the English admiral, Sydney Smith, established an observation post here in 1802.

The ancient town was about four to five times the size of that of the present day, and spread like an amphitheatre up towards Monte Smith. Italian architects identified the remains of a **temple of Athena Polias and Zeus Polias** on the northernmost point of the hill. The temple was one of the city's most important shrines. To the south are buildings that formed one of the centres of Rhodian intellectual and artistic life. The Italians also partially rebuilt a 3rd-century BC **Temple of Apollo**. It is thought that the original temple was destroyed by the same earthquake that destroyed the Colossus of Rhodes. Below the Temple of Apollo – which is still a landmark to ships at sea – is a heavily restored **stadium**. Only a few of the rows of seats are from the 2nd century BC.
To the north of the entrance to the stadium is a small **theatre**, also from the same period, and also partly restored. Its size indicates it was not the main theatre of the ancient city but

was once used for musical and other events in honour of Apollo. To the southwest of the stadium are **tombs** and remains of the city's outer walls.
Monte Smith offers excellent views over the whole northwest coast. The panorama is particularly delightful at dusk, when the lovely sunsets for which Rhodes is renowned can be enjoyed to the full.
You can get to Monte Smith on the No 5 bus which leaves from the station near the Néa Agorá (New Market). The journey takes about half an hour. A taxi ride to the site is not expensive.

◆◆
MOUSEÍO TIS KOSMIKÍS TÉCHNIS (MUSEUM OF DECORATIVE ARTS)

Platia Argirokástrou, Old Town
This folk-art museum contains local pottery, carpets, costumes and other domestic items. It is housed in what is thought to have been an arsenal. Of particular note is a reconstruction of a house interior. Featured are a loom and spinning wheel, a cradle and a woven baby-carrier. The fireplace has a cooking shelf set into it and on this are earthenware pitchers and other utensils. From the ceiling hangs a rush carrier to enable cheese to be kept well above floor level. Also of special interest is a glass case containing an impressive collection of plates and jugs from Nicaea (modern Iznik in Turkey), in the Rhodian style.
Open: 09.00–15.00hrs.
Closed: Mondays.

Adjoining the museum is the **Armeria Palace**, the earliest

The Temple of Apollo, Monte Smith, dates from the 3rd century BC

Infirmary of the Knights. Now occupied by the Institute of History and Archaeology, its upper gallery has an intriguing relief carving of an hourglass.

◆◆
MUNICIPAL GARDENS

New Town
Located beneath the Palace of the Grand Masters, the gardens are the scene of *son et lumière* performances ('Íchos kai Fos' in Greek) each evening in the summer, and are a pleasant spot for an evening stroll or as an escape from the heat of the midday sun.
The audio-visual interpretations of the rise and fall of the Crusaders' town begin at 20.15hrs and last approximately

45 minutes. An English language version is usually performed every night, except Sunday, with Swedish, German, French and Greek versions on alternative evenings, but it is wise to check schedules with the tourist office, since they can change.

◆◆

NEÁ AGORÁ (NEW MARKET)

New Town

This Turkish-style building faces Mandraki Harbour and encloses a large area crammed with fruit and vegetable stalls, fast food cafeterias, souvenir shops and, to one side of the tree-shaded internal courtyard, the raised rotunda building of the Fish Market. The shops which occupy the arcaded area facing the harbour are, in the main, cafés and cake shops, while liquor, grocery and gift shops, as well as a number of small supermarkets, can be found on the market's external periphery. Entry to the inner courtyard is through various alleyways that pierce the façade.

Taking a close look at the fishy business in the Néa Agorá

♦♦
RODHINÍ PARK
about 2 miles (3km) east of Rhodes Town
This forested park, landscaped by the Italians, is a delightful, shady spot with rose gardens, lakes with rustic bridges, a mass of oleander bushes, flowers, cypresses and maples. It is also the site of a 3rd-century BC necropolis, or cemetery, containing among other finds a tomb, carved in the rock, and decorated with half-columns in the Doric style. Traditionally known as the **Tomb of Ptolemy**, it dates from the Hellenistic period and was restored by the Italians in 1924. Ptolemy was the general of Alexander the Great. The park is also thought to have been the site of a School of Rhetoric, founded in the 4th century BC, where many famous figures in Greek and Roman history, including Julius Caesar, studied.
In the summer months musical performances of bouzouki and international music are a regular feature, and the park also contains an enclosure with Rhodian deer. There is also a pleasant garden restaurant with a nightclub.

SON ET LUMIÈRE see **MUNICIPAL GARDENS** page 29

♦♦♦
TURKISH QUARTER ✓
Old Town
The Turkish influence can be seen in the numerous minarets and arched windows built by the Turks after their conquest of Rhodes in 1522. The Christians of the island were given until sunset to leave the island, and their churches were speedily converted into mosques by the addition of minarets.

Muslim Islanders
Unlike mosques elsewhere in the Greek islands, some of those on Rhodes are still used by worshippers. Rhodes has quite a large Muslim population, dating from the 16th century conquest and boosted in 1913 by Greek and Turkish Muslims driven from their homes on Crete. The Neá Kritika (New Cretan) district on the road to the airport is still a largely Muslim community.

Near the **Mosque of Souleïmán** (see page 32) is the **Turkish Library** (Tourkikí Vivliothíki), containing valuable Turkish, Arab and Persian manuscripts. Of particular interest to the visitor are two beautifully decorated Korans, one dated 1412 and the other 1540. The library is housed in the rooms of the **Medresse Mosque** which was once a Greek church (dedicated to St George), and its attractive courtyard is decorated with pretty pebble mosaics. The **Mosque of the Aga** (Tzamí tou Aga), or Turkish commander, is located halfway down Odos Sokrátous and is unusual in that it is built on wooden, stilt-like legs. The **Retjep Pasha Mosque** (Tzamí Retset Pascha), on Odos Omírou, was once the most beautiful in Rhodes. Built in 1588 of material from several churches, it is now abandoned.

◆◆

TZAMÍ TOU MOURAD REÏS (MOSQUE OF MOURAD REÏS)

Plateía Koundouriótou New Town
Located next to the National Theatre, at Mandraki Harbour, the shimmering white minaret of this mosque is arguably the most elegant on the island. It is approached through a cemetery leading to a shady yard paved in black and white. The mosque is to the left, and the tomb of Mourad Reïs lies within a small circular building on the right. Mourad Reïs was one of Souleïmán's admirals and was killed during the final assault on Rhodes in 1521–2.
The cemetery, built in 1523, is planted with a multitude of eucalyptus trees and crowded with Turkish headstones – an evocative place, away from the tourist bustle.

◆◆

TZAMÍ SOULEÏMÁN (MOSQUE OF SOULEÏMÁN)

Odos Sokrátous, Old Town
Erected by Souleïmán the Magnificent to show his gratitude for the conquest of the Knights in 1522, this is the largest mosque in Rhodes and one of the few still used for worship. Its present-day appearance dates from 1808. The portal is thought to be from a church which once stood on the site. Inside, the mosque is spacious, quiet and pleasing, unlike most of the other mosques on the island, which are in a sorry state of neglect. It contains a stone minaret, red plaster walls and a Byzantine pulpit.
The mosque is unfortunately not open to visitors.

◆◆

WALLS, GATES AND MOATS

The medieval military walls, towers and gates of the old quarter of Rhodes Town were constructed by the Knights, who also excavated the ditches. They were built, in part, on Byzantine foundations. After 1464 the fortress was divided into eight bulwarks which were allocated, for defence purposes, to the eight Tongues. After repulsing the Turkish siege of 1480, Italian engineers were commissioned to assist the then Grand Master, Pierre d'Aubusson, to strengthen the fortifications which, in places, resulted in wall thicknesses up to 40 feet (12m). The number of gates was reduced and the moat widened to some 65 feet (20m). In the 15th century the existing walls were reconstructed and strengthened by the Knights to improve defences against the Turks.
Of the gates (*pýli*) in the walls the most impressive are: **Amboise Gate** (Pýli Ambouaz), one of the grandest of them all, it leads, via a triple-arched bridge, over the outer moat and through the main part of the gate, bedded in the enormous walls; **Liberty Gate** (Pýli Eleftherías), a narrow gap busy with tourists and traffic, it leads to Plateía Sýmis, containing a 3rd-century BC temple of Aphrodite.
Constructed as recently as 1924, the gate was renamed in 1947 on the reunification of the Dodecanese islands with Greece.
The Esplanade roadway skirts the Commercial Harbour and is dominated by massive walls

Pýli Eleftherias (Freedom Gate) commemorates Rhodes' liberation from foreign rule

which are pierced by three gates – **Arsenal** (Pýli tou Oplostasíou), **Harbour** (Pýli Limániou) and **St Catherine's** (Pýli Agia Ekaterínis). Particularly worthy of inspection is the bas-relief over the Harbour Gate. The battlements run from the Customs Hall Quay (Telonío) along the west side of the Acandia Harbour to the **Gate of Italy**, built in 1924. The **Gate of St Athanasius** (Pýli Agíou Athanassíou) was where Souleïmán the Magnificent breached the defences in 1522. Twice-weekly guided tours of the walls (Mondays and Saturdays) start at the Palace of the Grand Masters, and last about one and a half hours. Check with the tourist information office for details.

Accommodation

Most hotels and self-catering apartments in Rhodes Town are located in the New Town; visitors who want to stay in the more peaceful but mainly residential Old Quarter must look for *pensions* or private rooms (the tourist office will advise) although in high season these can be difficult to find. Odos Omírou and Odos Dilberaki are good places to look for cheap rooms.

Acandia Hotel, 61 Iroon Polytechniou (tel: 22251). A pleasant veranda where you can enjoy drinks or snacks is one of the features here. The 82 bedrooms all have private bath, balcony, telephone and radio. Grade B.

Athina Hotel, 27 Odos G Leon (tel: 22631). Situated in a central position close to the beach and all the town's amenities and nightlife, with lounge, bar, lifts, large swimming pool and solarium, and a breakfast room/restaurant. Grade B.

Belvedere, PO Box 144, Rhodes (tel: 24471). Only a short walk from the centre of Rhodes Town, this 165-room hotel overlooks a stretch of shingle and rocky beach, reached by subway. A modern, family-owned establishment on three floors, its facilities include a large, seawater pool with children's section, attractively furnished sun terraces, and a restaurant serving both Greek and international dishes. Grade A.

Blue Sky Hotel, Platia Psaropoulas (tel: 24091). Right on the seafront, about five minutes' walk from the town centre. All 182 bedrooms have central heating, telephone, three-channel music, private bathroom and balcony. Many have splendid sea views. Amenities include shops, a hairdresser's and a nightclub featuring live music and Greek folklore shows. Because of its location on the main road and near a busy roundabout, the Blue Sky is not the best choice for those with small children. Other disadvantages include three-sided lifts and indecipherable depth markings in the pool. Grade A.

Hotel Helena, 72 Odos G Griva (tel: 22681). Within a ten-minute walk of the centre of Rhodes Town, the Helena is a clean, highly recommended family-owned hotel offering excellent value for money. It has a small but clean seawater pool, good sun terrace, and an attractive breakfast room opening on to the pool terrace. Warning notices indicate that three-sided lifts are operated. Grade C.

Ibiscus Hotel, PO Box 90, 17 Odos Nisirou (tel: 29421). A friendly, modern hotel located across the road from the beach and about a mile (1.5km) from the centre of town, the Ibiscus offers a terrace, lounge, bar, two additional lounges, dining room, television room, card tables, and a popular steak house. Furniture is comfortable but somewhat basic. Grade A.

Lomeniz Hotel, Odos Cl Peper, Constadini (tel: 34649). This is a highly recommended, recent, 210-room hotel, located in a semi-residential area about a mile and a half (2.5km) from the centre of town but opposite a pleasant stretch of sandy beach. Facilities offered range from a swimming pool – rather small considering the hotel's size – bar, taverna, garden, and facilities for table tennis and billiards. A minus point is that the marble floors can be very slippery. Grade B.

Marie Hotel, 7 Odos Kos (tel: 30577). With a heated swimming pool and sauna, the Marie claims to offer A-grade facilities at C-grade prices. Its 125 rooms all have balconies, bathrooms, telephones and music channels, and the hotel is situated opposite the town's park, about 100 yards/metres from the beach. Apart from the swimming pool and sauna, other amenities include a bar, television lounge, pub and cafeteria. Grade C.

Mediterranean Hotel, 35–7 Odos Kos (tel: 24661). This is an elegant medium-sized hotel

enjoying a good location on the seafront opposite a busy stretch of shingle beach, and about ten minutes' walk from the bars, shops, restaurants and nightlife of the town centre. There is an attractively decorated lounge area, several bars, a large dining room, and an open-air patio with pleasant views. Grade A.
Park Hotel, 12 Odos Riga Ferreou (tel: 24611). In a quiet, residential quarter of Rhodes Town yet only a few minutes' walk from the beach, the Park offers a restaurant, bar, verandas, gardens, and a large swimming pool. Grade A.
Regina Hotel (tel: 22171). Centrally located in the town, it is close to all the amenities, and the beach is only six minutes along the road. Most of the 82 bedrooms have balconies and the hotel also has a breakfast room, television lounge, games room and a splendid roof-top bar with beautiful views across the harbour and town. Grade A.
Grand Hotel Astir Palace, 1 Odos Aktí Mioúti (tel: 26284). This long-established hotel has been brought back up to deluxe standards by the Astir chain. Conveniently located within easy walking distance of the centre of Rhodes Town, it stands in its own grounds just across the road from the beach, where windsurfing and pedaloes are available. The hotel also has two outdoor seawater pools. For evening entertainment there is an international casino – the only one on the island – and a nightclub, 'Isabella'. Sports facilities include a floodlit tennis court and a games room with table tennis and electronic games. Children have their own swimming pool. Deluxe.
Hotel Spartalis, 2 Odos N Plastíra (tel: 24371). Just a couple of minutes' walk from Mandraki Harbour and ten minutes' walk from the beach, the Spartalis provides a good base from which to explore the town and take day trips to other islands. The rooms, which have been renovated, are of a good size and half have balconies overlooking the harbour. There is no entertainment provided in this hotel, but all the facilities of the town are within walking distance. The hotel is comfortable and the management efficient and friendly. Grade B.
Stella Guest House, 58 Odos Dilveraki (tel: 24935). Charming and friendly, this small guest house is run by resident proprietors. Situated in the centre of the modern quarter of Rhodes Town, it is a few minutes' stroll from the nearest stretch of beach, and is a good choice for those on a tight budget. Grade B.

Restaurants

Rhodes Town offers an enormous choice of restaurants, tavernas, self-service cafeterias, take-away establishments, pastry shops, bars and cafés. Restaurants specialising in pizzas and pasta are everywhere, especially along Odos Orfanidou in the New Town, and are relatively inexpensive. Even cheaper are the restaurants within the New Market.

Recommendations

Kon-Tiki (tel: 22477). An upmarket floating restaurant located by the harbour jetty, the

Kon-Tiki is popular with those looking for an unusual setting, although it is not cheap.

Casa Castelana, 33 Odos Aristotelous in the Old Town (tel: 28803). Not cheap, but atmospheric, with a delightful walled garden for al fresco eating (evening reservations recommended). Located in a house built in 1480, it has been a restaurant for 16 years, offering a good range of fish and steak dishes, with specialities such as *trahanas*, a traditional village soup.

Both **Alexis** and **Fotis**, in Odos Sokrátous, in the Old Town, are renowned for their excellent, if pricey, fish dishes, while **Melas**, near the Palace of the Grand Masters, has good Greek cuisine, as does the moderately priced **Myconos**, in Odos Papanikoláou, New Town. Another New Town recommendation is the **Dania**, near the TUI office, which offers a cold Danish buffet every Sunday evening.

Romeo, 7-9 Odos Menekleou, specialises in Greek dishes and fresh seafood, with live traditional music every evening.

Palia Historia, at the corner of Mitropoleos and Dendrinou, is a great place to sample meze.

La Pizzaggio Pizzeria, Platia Ag. Nikolaos, has affordable pizzas and pasta and delivers to any address in town (tel: 24506).

Iguana, at Odos Anthoulas Zervou, behind the Blue Sky Hotel, specialises in Tex-Mex cooking – excellent chilli and margarita cocktails.

Salt & Pepper, Odos Michali Petridi, has superb mezes, grills and a wide range of vegetarian dishes. It has a good selection of Greek wines.

Self-service/Fast Food

For those on a budget or looking for an inexpensive meal, the numerous self-service restaurants and cafeterias are a good bet. Particularly recommended are the **Yellow Spot**, Odos G Griva; **Sally Brown's**, Odos 25 Martiou; and **Chevalier's Corner**, attached to the Chevalier's Palace Hotel. Of the numerous pizzerias in town, **La Pizzagio**, at the corner of Platia Ayios Nikólaos, is particularly good.

Coffee Shops, Bars, Pubs

There are atmospheric coffee shops throughout Rhodes Town, most of them frequented by locals, who linger over their pastries, small cups of sweet coffee and glasses of water, playing backgammon. Recommended coffee shops include **Trianon**, in Platia Akadimas; **Rendez-vous**, Iróon Polytechniou; and **Etanh**, in Odos Ammóchostou. Bars and pubs that are popular with locals as well as visitors include **Mango Bar**, Platia Douleios, **Belle Nuit**, Odos Orfeos; and the **White Rock Pub** in Odos Nikiforou Mandilara. **Nvn Ke Ai** is a stylish piano bar off the lower end of Odos Sokrátous in the Old Town.

Nightlife and Entertainment

Among the best discothèques and nightclubs are **Le Palais**, in Odos 25 Martiou, next to the main Post Office, which features an atmospheric piano bar, discothèque and restaurant; **Mercedes Play Boy**, Leoforos Ialyssou; **Obsession**, in the

Alexis, a splendidly preserved old luxury restaurant in the Old Town

Panagos shopping centre at Monte Smith; and **Sodoma**, in Leoforos Ialyssou.

Greek folk dancing can be enjoyed at numerous establishments, including the restaurant **Don Kichotis**, at 24 Odos Orfeos, in the Old Town.

Other places specialising in bouzouki or folk music include **Café Chantant**, 22 Odos Aristotelous, Old Town; **Melrose**, 12 Odos Riga Ferreou; **Rodos By Night**, opposite the Hotel Miramare, and the **Olympia** restaurant/coffee bar near the main Post Office. Greek dance and folk song performances are given every evening except Saturday from May to October at the **Old Town Theatre**, in the Old Town, (tel: 20157/29085).

Shopping

Anyone who likes shopping and window-browsing will enjoy Rhodes. There are shops, boutiques and mini-markets throughout the island, although most shoppers understandably make a bee-line for Rhodes Town, which has more than 4,000 shops situated in the modern shopping districts of the New Town area, and in the cobbled streets of the medieval walled city. The two markets (Palia Agorá and Néa Agorá) offer a variety of goods and plenty of local colour.

For information on good buys and where to make them, see the chapter **Shopping** pages 95–7.

LÍNDOS

Just 35 miles (56km) down the east coast from Rhodes Town, Líndos is the island's second most important tourist spot, popular both for day trips and as a place to stay.

Your first glimpse of Líndos – a National Historic Landmark and one of the most beautiful sites in Greece – is captivating . . . a cluster of small, dazzlingly white houses nestling on a hillside overlooking a curving bay of sparkling blue water and golden sand, crowned by a magnificent fortress. And despite the hordes of tourists who descend on Líndos each summer, the village remains charming, with a delightful labyrinth of narrow little alleyways which at times pass below shady canopies of vines.

As you look down on this little village and the bay, or up at the imposing acropolis, bear in mind that this was once a city famous for its commerce, its riches, its temples and its seamen, with a population at one time of 17,000, compared with today's 700 inhabitants.

St Paul visited Líndos, landing, it is believed, at the little bay below the southern slopes of the acropolis. Then, in the Byzantine period, the acropolis was fortified, first by the Byzantines and then by the Knights of St John, during whose time on the island the fortresses of Líndos, Feráklos and Ialyssós were the strongest outside Rhodes Town.

Líndos was excavated by Danish archaeologists early this century, while restoration work on the buildings in the acropolis was undertaken by the Italians. The village at the foot of the acropolis lies on the site of the ancient city, which seems to have been abandoned between the 6th and 10th centuries AD when the inhabitants went to live on the acropolis. It began to be re-inhabited in the 11th century and subsequently knew times of great fortune.

Safe Haven

Líndos possesses the only natural harbour on the island, which is presumably why it developed into, and remained, the most important of Rhodes' three great ancient cities – and an important commercial city of antiquity. It first appeared in history about the time of the Dorians, although there is evidence there was a Minoan settlement here prior to this period. Because the land surrounding Líndos is not the most fertile on the island, its inhabitants turned towards the sea for their livelihood, becoming traders and fishermen, and Lindian sailors explored and colonised as far away as Italy, France and Spain.

Today Líndos enjoys a different kind of prosperity, as a holiday mecca. The sandy beach fringing the main bay is popular with youngsters and families, being gently shelving into the sea and offering safe bathing. It is ideal for learning to windsurf or waterski, and for those who simply wish to laze around and sunbathe the surrounding scenery is magnificent. A small, rocky outcrop separates the main bay from Pallas Beach,

The acropolis of Líndos, with its medieval walls, overlooks one of the island's prettiest bays.

which is smaller but also sandy. Shops, tavernas and bars cluster around the main square and in the narrow alleyways and tiny, cobbled streets. Líndos has been declared an official archaeological site, and permission must be sought to make any repairs, changes, improvements or even to paint window shutters of its buildings. Notwithstanding the restrictions, former fishermen's houses have been converted into souvenir shops, bars or apartments, and though Líndos remains delightful, little of its traditional feel persists.

WHAT TO SEE

◆◆◆
ACROPOLIS ✓

For a superb view of the village, the beach and the tiny harbour of St Paul, you will need to climb the uneven steps to the hill-top fortress built in the Middle Ages by the Knights of St John, around the ancient acropolis. From here you can gaze down on the beach, crowded with sun-worshippers, the bay alive with windsurfers, and waterskiers. The walk up to the acropolis from the main square is not that long or precipitous, so save your drachmas and the backs of the

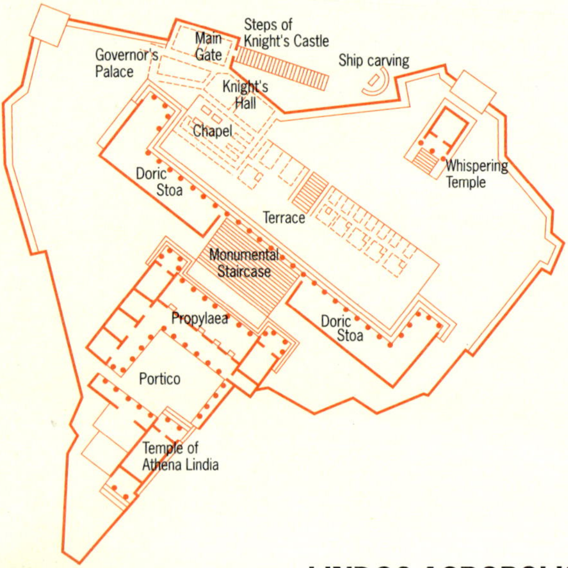

LINDOS ACROPOLIS

Stone Ship
Whether you climb the acropolis on foot or by donkey, it is worth stopping to look at an unusual **rock carving** *en route*; thought to have been part of the base for a statue of a priest of Poseidon called Aghesandros, it represents the almost life-size stern of a Hellenistic ship complete with poop and steering paddles. The inscription tells us it was the work of the sculptor Pythokritos in the 2nd century BC.

little donkeys, and walk up. Other rocks along the route are used by local women to display their crochet work and embroidered goods.

The final stage of the ascent is up a flight of steps leading through the main doorway into a vaulted hall above which, in medieval times, was the governor's palace. The gateway and hall were built by the Knights, and the hall is used for an informal display of Classical and Hellenistic pieces. Once through the hall you emerge into a paved yard. Turn left through a medieval, barrel-vaulted chamber and you come out into the lowest of the four terraces which, one above the other, mount to the temple. On this level the outer walls are on your left and some open storehouses on your right. There are also traces of a Doric and Corinthian temple at this level. Possibly dating from Roman times, it is popularly known as the **Whispering Temple**.

On the next level, reached by a short stairway, is the Doric stoa of the **Temple of Athena Lindia**, stretching some 100 yards (90m) on either side as you face it. The portico, or arcade, originally had 42 columns, of which 20 are now standing. The eight central columns of the façade stand in front of a monumental staircase leading to the propylaea (entrance). The small but elegant temple is thought to have been rebuilt after a fire in 345 BC. It stands at the edge of a cliff which drops nearly 400 feet (120m) to the sea below, and was built in the Doric style, but with columns only at the front and rear, unlike most temples of the period.

A temple containing a statue of Athena is known to have existed here in the 10th century BC. By the middle of the 6th century BC an elaborate stone temple was erected by the then tyrant, Kleoboulus, but this building was later destroyed and the statue with it. In 348 BC the Lindians themselves built a temple and put into it a new statue of Athena, fashioned of wood, gold, marble and ivory, and wearing a wreath instead of a helmet. This house of the goddess Athena became one of the most important religious centres in Greece and the Mediterranean. It came to an end at the hands of the Emperor Theodosius of Byzantium, who removed to Constantinople many of its treasures, including the statue of the goddess.

The acropolis was used in Classical times both for ceremony

The acropolis looks down on the sea once sailed by the ancient ship shown in Pythokritos's carving

and as a refuge for the people in times of war. The Knights of St John saw both advantages, though its real importance was as a military stronghold of the Order second only to Rhodes Town itself. The Grand Master, Foulques de Villaret, took sanctuary here when he was ousted from the office in 1317.

After the Knights departed from Rhodes the Turks took over and in the middle of the 19th century they built houses on the acropolis and lodged a garrison there.

Open: daily 08.30–17.00hrs.
Closed: Mondays.

◆◆◆
LINDIAN HOUSES
Líndos is full of attractive, whitewashed houses, many dating from the 17th century and some built in Gothic style with Byzantine or oriental decoration. The oldest house is inscribed with the date 1599. Many of the houses are topped with small rooms to enable the owners to have a view of their ships in the harbour, and are known as the Houses of the Captains. Some have been restored and their interiors preserved as folk museums. The tourist information office in the main square will give further information on which houses are open to visitors.

The Good House
Lindian houses are solidly built, embellished with decorations of Byzantine doves, peacocks and flowers, or rope or chain patterns. Their interiors are characterised by high, wooden ceilings painted with floral designs, and their courtyards paved in decorative black and white *chochlaki* (pebble mosaic).
Some of the houses built since the 16th century are distinguished by a large, rectangular room known as 'the good house'. This contains a wide arch spanning nearly the full width of one wall, within which is built a long, low platform, reached by a flight of three steps – the family bed, generally covered with rugs with boldly embroidered pillows heaped in either corner. The wall above the bed platform is usually hung with Lindian plates and embroidered cloths.

◆◆
ÓRMOS LÍNDOS (ST PAUL'S BAY)
A small bay surrounded by bare rock, this is the spot where, it is claimed, a bolt of lightning and a clap of thunder caused the rock to split asunder creating a harbour that enabled a storm-tossed boat, bearing St Paul on one of his evangelising journeys, to reach safety. His arrival in AD 51 is considered to be when Christianity reached the island and has given rise to the annual festival of St Paul here on 28 and 29 June.

◆◆
PANAGÍA (CHURCH OF THE ASSUMPTION OF OUR LADY)
Located near the main square, and dominating the centre of Líndos, this delightful church has well-preserved frescoes by Gregory Simi depicting well-known biblical scenes. They were painted in 1779 but restored in 1927. In one, St Francis is shown with the head of an ass. Above the main door is a delightful sequence showing people being weighed in the scales. Those found wanting are shown descending to hell, while the righteous are being elevated on little clouds. The 17th-century wooden sanctuary screen and bishop's throne are finely carved, and the floor is of black and white pebble mosaic, traditional to the Dodecanese islands. At the far end of the church is a burial chamber for priests and certain citizens. A number of 17th-century icons inside are well worth inspecting, notably the three immediately above the door. The centre one

Órmos Líndos is a small calm bay separated from Líndos by the acropolis headland

is of the Virgin and Child enclosed in a painted arc; on the left is a fine composition believed to be of an angel blessing a dying man in the presence of the prophet David with his harp and a company of angels. All the icons were the gifts of Lindians to the memory of relatives buried in the room. The church is possibly older than the inscription of 1484–90, which could refer to a period of rebuilding by the Knights.

◆◆◆
THEATRE ✓

The theatre of the ancient city is located on the western slope of the acropolis, facing the sea, and dates from the 4th century BC. The amphitheatre is in fair condition – five of the gangways are clearly visible and four climb up through the lower seats to the higher ones. There is a decorated gangway dividing the two banks of seats. The lower bank is of 20 rows and at ground level there is the customary front row of stone chairs for the priests and other dignitaries. As you face the theatre, an excavated area marks the site of an ancient temple, possibly dedicated to Apollo. Later, a Byzantine chapel was built on the site, but this was demolished at the beginning of World War II.

◆◆

TOMB OF KLEOBOULUS

Located near the northeast end of the harbour, looking down over the village, this is a giant, circular Hellenistic chamber made from square stone slabs. It dates possibly from the 5th or 4th century BC. It was later converted into a Christian church. Kleoboulus was a 6th-century tyrant leader of Líndos, who ruled for 40 years and was one of the Seven Sages of the ancient world.

Accommodation

Because Líndos is an official archaeological site and a conservation area, there are no hotels in the village itself, only small *pensions* and village rooms. These tend to be simple in the extreme, often verging on the basic, with few luxuries or modern furnishings. Many have what are described by tour operators as double bunker beds – a raised wooden platform on which there are either two separate mattresses or a double mattress. This is a layout typical of Líndos and traditional Lindian houses. The nearest hotels lie outside the village, at **Vliha Beach**, about 15 minutes' walk away.

Atmospheric traditional Líndos villas, studios and apartments

The secluded Líndhos Bay Hotel

can be rented through Direct Greece, Putney Bridge Approach, London SW6 3JT (tel: (0171-371 9595).

Hotel Yiota Beach (tel: 42205). This is a friendly, small, family-run hotel located next to a lovely stretch of beach. Although facilities are limited, guests are welcome to use those of the Líndos Bay Hotel – about 300 yards (270m) away – and Steps of Líndos, which is about three quarters of a mile (1km) away. The hotel's popular **Akrogiali** taverna/restaurant is open all day and offers a range of snacks and meals. Breakfast is served either in the taverna or out on the patio. Grade B.

Líndhos Bay Hotel (tel: 42211/2). This large hotel is set on its own fine shingle beach, and offers a saltwater swimming pool with sun terrace, shops, restaurant and snack bar, tennis courts and table tennis facilities, and fortnightly Greek evenings in the high season. Cots and high chairs are available on request, but on a negative note the three-sided lifts carry no warning notices of possible danger. The management operates a mini-bus service to and from Líndos several times a day. Grade A.

Líndhos Sun Hotel (tel: 31453). Situated five minutes' walk from a stretch of dark, coarse sand, this is a small, friendly hotel offering lovely sea and mountain views. However, the walk to Líndos is up a steep road, making this an unsuitable choice for those with walking difficulties. Facilities include a large, freshwater swimming pool with poolside bar. Grade C.

Hotel Steps of Líndhos (tel: 42262). Located about ten minutes' walk down a fairly steep hill to a sand-and-shingle stretch of beach, the many traditionally styled three-storey accommodation blocks of the hotel are set into a hillside, affording magnificent views across Vliha Bay. Facilities include stylishly furnished and comfortable public rooms, a lounge/reception area, main lounge bar opening on to a terrace, outdoor swimming pool set in sun terraces, separate children's pool, a poolside bar/restaurant, and shops selling newspapers, souvenirs and jewellery. For children the amenities range from a paddling pool and playground, to high chairs, free cots, and babysitting on request. For those who enjoy sport there is a tennis court, table tennis, and various watersports near by, including waterskiing, windsurfing and pedaloes. The hotel has a quiet, relaxing atmosphere, making it suitable for families and older couples. Guests here also need to be fit, since there are numerous steps to negotiate – and no lifts. Grade A.

Restaurants and Entertainment

Líndos offers a large selection of tavernas, restaurants and lively bars to suit all tastes. The **Taverna Mihalis**, located near the ancient theatre, specialises in grilled meat and chicken, and has a pleasant rooftop terrace, while the **Lindian Apollo** cafeteria/pub, which also has an attractive roof garden, offers a variety of cocktails, including

Eye-catching local pottery from Líndos is a good souvenir

some with the most startling names. The **Antika** cocktail bar is spacious and stylishly furnished. There are also a couple of discothèques, situated on the outskirts of the village.

Shopping
Líndos is famous for its pottery, especially plates, which make excellent wall decorations and good souvenirs. Lindian pottery was first made in the 16th century AD. It is said that the Knights of St John captured a ship carrying Persian craftsmen and held them on Rhodes, where they taught the art of pottery. The best plates were made in the 16th and 17th centuries, as is shown from the large number of examples on display in the Benaki Museum, Athens.

Other Facilities

Bank: the National Bank is close to the main square, off Odos Akrópoli. (*Open*: Mondays to Thursdays 09.00–14.00hrs; Friday 09.00–13.30hrs; Saturday – summer only 09.00–13.30hrs.)

Buses: the large square at the edge of the village serves as the bus terminal.

Clinic: to the left of Odos Akrópoli, opposite the donkey park (tel: 31224).

Ferry-boats: an excursion boat departs from Grand Harbour Bay daily in summer at 14.30hrs for Rhodes Town.

Police: at the further end of Odos Akrópoli.

Post Office: close to the donkey marshalling yard on Odos Akrópoli, near the main square.

Toilets: a public lavatory is located by the main square.

Tourist Office: in Platia Eleftherios. (*Open*: daily 09.00–10.00hrs and 17.00–20.00hrs.)

OTHER RESORTS AND SITES

◆◆

AFÁNTOU

east coast

Afántou means 'hidden place' or 'invisible' and it is indeed set back some way from the coast. It is a pleasant resort, much quieter and more select than Faliráki or Ixós. However, buses run from the village along the coast road and there are taxis. Afántou retains a traditional village atmosphere, and you will see locals sipping ouzo and playing backgammon outside the tavernas there. The beach is a fairly peaceful stretch of coarse sand and shingle, with secluded rocky inlets. Beach umbrellas and sunbeds are readily available. A handful of tavernas and bars can be found along the main road. Afántou is particularly popular with golfers, since it has an excellent 18-hole golf course.

Accommodation

Hotel Golden Days (tel: 51659). This simple, unsophisticated family-run hotel, built in 1986, stands just outside the village and enjoys lovely countryside and sea views. Amenities include a small reception area combined with a lounge/bar and a breakfast room. Grade C.

Xenia Afandou (tel: 51121). An attractive, 52-bed hotel in the golf course grounds and bordering the beach. It offers no fewer than three swimming pools. Grade B.

There is a reasonable selection of tavernas as well as several coffee shops and a bakery around the village square.

◆◆◆

ARCHÁNGELOS

east coast, 20 miles (33km) from Rhodes Town

This is the largest village on the island and, although not overly attractive, is pleasantly situated within the principal citrus-growing region on the island. It is worth visiting if only for the potteries here which specialise in hand-thrown ceramics, especially plates, and for the hand-made leather boots. The village, on the coast road, lies in the shadow of a ruined 15th-century fortress commissioned by Grand Knight Master Orsini. There are three churches and the village contains an interesting and atmospheric old quarter.

Load of Old...

Local cobblers in Archángelos still make traditional leather boots originally worn as protection against snakes. Women's boots appear to be made in two pieces – the top half overlaps the instep and ankle, giving the impression that there is a separate boot or shoe beneath. In fact the boots are all one piece, coming to well above the knee, with the surplus in a fold over the base of the heel. They are made of tough,hard-working hide or very soft goatskin.

Accommodation

Archángelos has few large hotels. The biggest is the Grade C **Tsampíka Sun** (tel: 22568), with 46 rooms. Smaller places include the Grade C **Anagros** (tel: 22248) and the Grade C **Anthi Sun** (tel: 22619), both with 14 rooms.

RÓDOS
Ródos
Akra Zonári
Kritiká
Kantíli
Rodiní
Sgouroú
Akra Vodí
Thérmes Kalithéa
Órmos Triánta
Ixiá
Ialyssós
Koskinoú
Moní Eleoúsas
Faliráki
Akra Ladikó
Órmos Afántou
Triánta
Kremastí
Pastída
267m Filérimos
Maritsá
Kalithiés
Koumoúli
Psalída
Afántou
Kolympia
Akra Vágia
Moní Tsampíka
Tsampíka
Archángelos
Stégna
Akra Archángelos
Paradeísi
Damatría
Petaloúdes
Psínthos
Loútani
Eptá Pigés
512m Profítis Ilías
Archipolí
551m Messóvouna
Theológos
Epáno Kalamónas
Moní Ag Kalopetra
480m Psínthos
Eleoússa
Platánia
Plataneró
Malónas
Másari
Makáris
Soroní
Fánes
Dimyliá
Ágios Nikólaos Fountoúkli
Apóllona
Kalavárda
Sálakos
798m Profítis Ilías
367m Assoúri
Moní Artamýti
Kameíros
Kapí
Akra Minás
Nánoi
Empónas
1215m Attávyros
Mandrikó
Kameíros Skála
Kritiniá
Kástellos
Amartoú
Lakkí
Glyfáda
Órmos Glyfáda
Mákri
Strongýli
Tragoússa
Alimiá
Chálki

Feráklos
Charáki
Akra Aimilianós
Órmos Vlika
Akrópoli
Órmos Líndos
Líndos
Akra Lárdos
Pefka
Kálathos
Pilóna
Órmos Lárdos
Gaïdouras
Lárdos
Moní Ipsenís
Láerma
Moní Thári
Asklipeio
Kontári
Gennádio
Moní Agíou Georgíou
Akra Lachaniá
Váti
585m
Profilia
Ágios Isídoros
Ístrios
Arníthia
Koukouliári
563m
Mesanagrós
Lachaniá
Chochlakás
Plimíri
Siána
Monólithos
Apolakkiá
Moní Skiádi
Kattavía
Ágios Pávlos
Akramytis
Monólithos Kástellos
319m
Órmos Apolakkiás
Akra Armenistís
Strongýlo
Chtenía
Karavólas
Akra Prasonísi
0
5
10 km

♦♦♦
EPTÁ PIGÉS (SEVEN SPRINGS) ✓

about 18 miles (30km) from Rhodes Town

Just off the main east coast road leading to Líndos, Eptá Pigés is one of the island's premier beauty spots – a pleasant place

The clear green lake at Eptá Pigés is said to be fed by seven springs

with a lake fed by seven streams, and a waterfall. It is a popular destination with excursion groups. To reach the lake you can take either a woodland trail or walk through a long, narrow, stream-running tunnel – an odd and unusual experience, and not one to be recommended to the claustrophobic; the tunnel is pitch-black, and the traffic two-way and chaotic. It is safe to swim in the lake, but not to get too close to the wall of the dam.

Restaurant

There is a restaurant, specialising in charcoal grills, some of whose tables are supported on flat-topped rocks in and alongside the water, all set in wooded countryside.

♦♦♦
FALIRÁKI

northeastern coast, about 9 miles (15km) from Rhodes Town

A long sweep of coarse, grey sand sloping gently to the sea is undoubtedly what has turned Faliráki into one of Rhodes' liveliest and most popular summer resorts – a far cry from the small fishing village it once was. Faliráki offers plenty to keep visitors occupied both on and off the beach. Sunbathing is good, swimming is safe, and the wide selection of watersports available includes windsurfing, parascending, waterskiing, jet-skiing and pedaloes. The resort also offers a mini-golf course and a go-kart track. The beach can – and, indeed usually does – get crowded in high season near the village, but a short walk further along will bring you to a quieter spot. As well as innumerable large hotels (with more being built), Faliráki has plenty of seaside amenities such as restaurants with rooms to let, changing cabins, showers, deck-chairs and parasols.

Accommodation

Faliráki contains a number of huge hotel complexes, such as the **Esperides Beach**, **Blue Sea** and **Rodos Beach**, which border the beach. At the far end of the bay are several smaller, more Greek-style establishments, together with a number of self-catering villas some of which, it should be noted, are located on the wrong side of the very busy main road.

Hotel Apollo Beach (tel: 85535). Standing in its own fresh, green gardens right beside Faliráki's

Faliráki beach is one of the best on the island

gently shelving sandy beach, and next door to the Faliráki Beach Hotel, this somewhat impersonal, 293-room establishment is close to the resort's tavernas and discos. It offers comfortable accommodation and good food, even if overall standards have declined slightly in recent years. Amenities include an outdoor freshwater pool, sun terraces, lounge, television and card rooms, bar, restaurant serving table d'hôte and à la carte dishes, taverna, hairdressing and beauty salons, and a gift shop. There are tennis courts with equipment for hire, a sauna, table tennis and billiards. For children there is a swimming pool, playground, high chair and cots, and baby-sitting on request. Grade A.

Hotel Blue Sea (tel: 85512). This 302-room hotel stands about a mile (1.6km) from the village. It has comfortable rooms, a good reputation for food and service, and gardens which border a lovely wide stretch of sand and pebble beach. A regular bus service to Rhodes Town stops outside the hotel. Amenities include outdoor and indoor swimming pools, jacuzzi, three lounges, bar, two tennis courts, squash court, pool table, live music three nights a week and a regular Greek night, shops, and a hairdresser. There is also a children's pool and small playground. Grade A.

Hotel Calypso (tel: 85455). Step through the gardens of the stylish Calypso and you are right on Faliráki's beach. The attractive terraces are equally inviting to sunbathers, and there is a good sized children's pool and play area. Other features include a saltwater swimming pool with poolside snackbar; tennis court and crazy-golf course; games room with billiards table; weekly discothèque and fortnightly Greek evenings; shops; beauty salon; sauna and gymnasium. The hotel's disadvantage is that it is in a somewhat isolated position, about 25 minutes' walk from the centre of the resort, but to compensate it is very smartly furnished and decorated and well recommended. Grade A.

Hotel Colossos Beach (tel: 85524). This hotel is a good choice for families, offering a wealth of facilities including its own stretch of private sand-and-shingle beach. Situated just over two miles (3km) from the centre of Faliráki, the hotel features a lounge, three bars, television room with satellite programmes, shops, a hairdressing salon, beauty salon, a main swimming pool and a children's pool, surrounded by terraces, extensive gardens, a poolside bar, and a beach bar. There are two restaurants offering a choice of menus, a cafeteria, à la carte taverna, and self-service poolside restaurant. There is dancing most nights in the 'Ace' discothèque, with regular live music sessions, and frequent Greek evenings are held in the taverna. There is also a programme of games and

Parasols at Faliráki: splashes of colour before a splash in the sea

competitions. Visitors with children should note that the lifts here are of the potentially dangerous, three-sided variety. Grade A.

Esperides Beach (tel: 85503). Dominating popular Faliráki bay and surrounded by a huge garden, this is a large, modern, highly recommended complex that includes three swimming pools, restaurant, cocktail bar, lounge, bridge room, television room, taverna, snack bar and discothèque. There is also a mini-market, hairdressing salon, car/bicycle rental office, and an excellent children's playground – one of the best on the island. The hotel is situated about 30 minutes' walk from the centre of Faliráki, but compensates for its somewhat isolated position with a very lively entertainment programme that includes party nights and Greek evenings. Its excellent facilities are marred slightly by the use of three-sided lifts. Grade A.

Esperos Palace Hotel (tel: 85734). Situated right on the beach, the stylish and elegant Esperos Palace has earned a reputation as one of the best hotels in Rhodes since its opening in 1985. Set in extensive gardens, it is linked by a bridge in the grounds to its sister hotel, Esperides Beach, whose facilities are shared. The hotel's 397 rooms are in two blocks connected by an art gallery corridor, and all are air-conditioned and have balconies with sea or garden views, larger-than-average bathrooms, self-dialling telephones, and mini-fridges. Facilities include two swimming pools with sun terraces, gardens, a piano bar, lounge bar, snack bar, boutique, mini-market and à la carte restaurant. There are also two tennis courts, squash courts, mini-golf course, and facilities for billiards. Grade A.

Faliráki Beach Hotel (tel: 85301). Recently renovated, this impressive and attractive hotel stands in a good position right in front of Faliráki's wide beach, reached through attractive gardens. Bars, tavernas and restaurants are all around, and shops, buses and taxis less than a minute's walk away. The resort centre is five minutes' walk away. Hotel facilities include a large outdoor swimming pool, sun terraces with chairs and umbrellas, poolside bar, lounge, bar, card room, restaurant, à la carte taverna and hairdressing salon. Occasional Greek evenings are held by the pool-side or in the bar, and for sports enthusiasts the hotel has two tennis courts, with equipment for hire, table tennis and putting, and there is golf available at Afántou, about four miles (6.5km) away. Children have their own pool and small playground, and high chairs, cots and early meals are available. Grade A.

Faliro Hotel (tel: 26511). For those on a budget, this small hotel is extremely popular, mainly thanks to the hospitality shown by Yiannis, his wife and their three children who make guests feel part of the family. There are tavernas and shops practically on the doorstep, the beach is about five minutes' walk away, and there is a bus stop close by for trips into Rhodes

Town. Breakfast is served on the outside terraced area of the bar. Grade D.
Pension Nefeli (tel: 85658). Another popular choice with those on a tight budget, the Nefeli is a small but pleasant property situated in a central position close to local shops, bars and tavernas and only ten minutes' stroll from a good stretch of beach. Facilities include a bar, lounge, and breakfast room. Grade C.
Hotel Rodos Beach (tel: 85412). This attractive and well-maintained hotel has a reputation for friendly service. Situated by the beach, where waterskiing and windsurfing are available in high season, it is just over a mile (1.6km) from Faliráki village. The comfortable, well-furnished bedrooms are in either the main building or bungalows in the hotel's large and pleasant gardens which border the beach. There is a saltwater swimming pool with sun terrace, poolside taverna with à la carte menu, beach bar, free tennis and table tennis, nightly discothèque, shops and hairdressing salon and a children's pool and playground. Three-sided lifts are used here, carrying warnings that children must be accompanied by an adult. Grade A.
Hotel Sun Palace (tel: 85650). This is a good quality hotel enjoying a relatively quiet location along a flat road about 20 minutes' walk from the resort centre and about 10 minutes' walk from the beach across a busy road. Facilities include a large, Olympic-sized freshwater swimming pool set in sun terraces, a poolside bar, principal bar, modern lounge areas and a card room. The hotel offers two restaurants featuring a weekly à la carte lunchtime poolside buffet and weekly buffet-style dinners, and regular entertainment ranges from Greek nights to discos. Other facilities include tennis courts, mini-golf and table tennis. Three-sided lifts used here carry no warnings, and there are no depth markings in the swimming pool. Grade A.

Restaurants and Entertainment

As in most seaside resorts, the road that leads down to the beach is where you will find the majority of the bars, tavernas, snack bars and shops. Although menus tend to cater more for international tastes, traditional cuisine can still be enjoyed at a few places. The **Acrogiali** Greek taverna bordering the beach has a good selection of Greek speciality dishes, including moussaka and squid. **Chaplin's Bar**, near by, is very lively in the evenings, and the popular cocktail bars include **Falirala** and **Blue Waves**, both near the beach, and the **Bianco Bar**, on the approach road.
Nightlife in Faliráki is very lively. From sunset the bars in the main street are packed with people – usually youngsters – enjoying themselves drinking and listening to the latest sounds. The most popular discothèques are **Buskers**, which has a weekly toga party, and **The Set**, just as lively but with a slightly more sophisticated atmosphere.

◆◆◆
IALYSSÓS ✓

about 6 miles (10km) southwest of Rhodes Town

The ancient city of Ialyssós occupies a plateau at the top of the 876-foot (267m) high Mount Filérimos, near the small but fast-developing west coast resort of Triánta. According to myth, the city was founded by Ialyssós, the third of the three grandsons of the sun god Helios. The earliest settlers here were the Phoenicians, followed by the Mycenaean Achaeans, who arrived from the Greek mainland about 1450 BC and named the place Achaea. The Dorians, under whom it grew to a city-state equalling Líndos and Kameíros in importance, named it after its mythical founder. With a commanding view of the island and the coast, the site has an obvious strategic value. Some time during the Dorian period the city began to edge down the western slopes of the hill

Fresco, Agios Georgios, Ialyssós

Church of Our Lady of Filérimos

towards Kremastí and Triánta. In this area an enormous necropolis containing numerous tombs was excavated by the French archaeologist Salzmann and British consul Biliotti between 1859 and 1871. They unearthed many finds now on display in museums throughout the world. In 1914 and again between 1929 and 1932 the Italians Majuri and Jacopi, in the course of fresh excavations, unearthed more new graves with rich finds from the Archaic, Classical and Hellenistic periods. The Knights of St John built a monastery and a church at Ialyssós. The monastery one sees today – with a courtyard surrounded by cells – was rebuilt by the Italians.

What to See

Chapel of Agios Georgios
Almost every inch of wall space in this small, subterranean Byzantine church is covered with frescoes of the 14th and 15th centuries. Some have been removed to reveal part of a Christian cross carved in stone beneath the plaster. Among the most interesting of the frescoes are a sequence of Grand Masters Kneeling Before Christ, a St George, and also a well-preserved series of incidents in the life of Christ which compose the decoration of the barrel vault.

Church of Our Lady of Filérimos
This is the first building most visitors to Ialyssós encounter after leaving the car park. Heavily restored after World War II, it was built on a site occupied, successively, by a Phoenician temple, a 3rd-century BC Doric temple to Athena Polias, an Early Christian basilica, a Catholic church converted from an Orthodox original, a restored 20th-century version of the church, and finally the present-day restoration. The chapel, built by d'Aubusson when he was the Knights' Grand Master, leads to two smaller chapels. On the floor of the rear of the church is a little red mosaic fish, part of the floor of the original Early Christian

building. There are two altars in the adjacent chapels, one for Catholic, the other for Orthodox worship, but only the latter is used today.

Cloisters

Beyond the church are the courtyards, galleries and cloisters of the monastery, somewhat heavily restored during the Italian occupation of Rhodes this century. The monks' cells are distinguished from one another by tiled plaques, each depicting a different flower.

Doric Fountain

Over the crest of the hill to the right of the monastery entrance, a flight of steps leads down to a 4th-century Classical fountain screened by a row of Doric columns, and discovered by accident in 1926. Once considered a sacred spring, it has since dried up. The Italians restored two of the six columns which had supported the roof of the portico and which was damaged by a landslide.

Icons in Golgothas recall the Passion

Stations of the Cross

A tree-lined avenue leading from the car park, and known as Golgothas, is lined on one side with 14 copper icons representing the stations of the cross, erected during the Italian occupation. At the end of the avenue, steps lead to a circular vantage point commanding breathtaking views along the coast. A mass of flowers in summer make it a popular spot with photographers.

A souvenir and drinks kiosk on the edge of the car park sells the liqueur Sette Erbe (Seven Herbs), which is made by monks.

Temple of Athena and Zeus Polias

Dating from the 3rd century BC, this Doric temple runs north and south in front of the Church of Our Lady of Filérimos. Foundations, bases, stumps of fluted pillars are all there, but little else. The temple was similar in style to the temple of Athena at Líndos, but much larger.

Open: daily 08.30–17.00hrs. *Closed*: Mondays.

Accommodation

Hotel Blue Horizon (tel: 93484). Commanding magnificent sea views, with the Turkish coast on the horizon, the hotel is well located on a stretch of sand-and-shingle beach, reached through well-tended lawns and gardens. The large gardens contain a swimming pool and sun terraces, while other hotel facilities include a restaurant,

Ixós – miles of sand, sea and surf

lounge, bar, snack bar, television and card room, shop, and hairdressing salon. Regular Greek folklore evenings are staged, while for children there is a separate pool and a playground. High chairs are available, as are early meals if a sufficient number of children are staying. Grade A.
Other hotel accommodation can be found in nearby **Triánta** (see separate entry).

Restaurant
The **Sandy Beach** taverna-coffee bar serves Greek dishes, with barbecued meat and fish as particular specialities.

◆◆
IXÓS (IXIÁ)
northwest coast
The lively, highly developed resort of Ixós is less than three miles (5km) along the main road from Rhodes Town, and separated from it only by the headland known as Monte Smith. It is tailor-made for the young, with countless bars, tavernas, cafeterias, discos and nightclubs packing this stretch of coastline and offering almost non-stop entertainment. Ixós enjoys a near constant breeze, making even the hottest days

feel comfortable. At times the wind can become very fresh, though umbrellas to act as wind-breaks are available for hire. Being only three miles (5km) from the island's airport, the resort does suffer from some aircraft noise, but this generally is not sufficiently annoying to detract from the enjoyment of a holiday here.

There are excellent facilities on the long, narrow beach of dark sand, shingle and pebble, with windsurfing particularly to be recommended from all the watersports on offer. Pedaloes are also available for hire, as are jet-skis, yachts and motor boats. The road along this stretch of the coast is busy most of the day, making it important to watch for children's safety, and the sea itself is not as calm as on the east coast.

Snacks, freshwater showers and sunbeds are all available on the beach, which is especially popular with early morning joggers. The resort also offers a children's playground, while several hotels have good sports facilities, including tennis courts, mini-golf courses and table tennis.

Accommodation

Avra Beach Hotel (tel: 25284/25308). Surrounded by a large garden, the hotel offers a wealth of amenities that range from a small shopping centre to children's swimming pool, kindergarten, hairdresser, car rental office, restaurant, open bar, and discothèque. Grade A.

Cosmopolitan Hotel (tel: 26473). This new hotel is positioned across the road from the seafront and only a short walk from the resort's beach. The centre of Ixós is a ten-minute walk away. A feature of the hotel is a huge, freshwater swimming pool flanked by spacious sun terraces, and there is also a separate pool for children. The attractive public areas include an excellent lounge and bar. Early suppers and children's menus are available. Grade A.

Hotel Dionyssos (tel: 23021). A sprawling complex of three buildings, the Dionyssos is situated three minutes from the beach, well back from the busy coast road, and offers spacious grounds together with two large pools – one with a children's section – poolside bar and gardens, and a children's playground. Other facilities include a 300-seat cinema and two bars. Notices warn of the possible danger posed by the hotel's three-sided lifts. Grade A.

Hotel Elina (tel: 92944). The Elina is particularly popular with Dutch and German visitors to the island. Standing in extensive grounds which border the sand-and-pebble beach, about 25 minutes' walk from the resort centre and about three miles (5km) along the coast from Rhodes Town, it has a spacious reception lobby with comfortable lounge area; bar; card tables; shops; a hairdressing salon; a large swimming pool set in extensive sun terraces and lawns; and a poolside bar with self-service snacks available at lunchtimes. Most bedrooms have pleasant sea views. For toddlers, cots are available, as are high chairs and children's menus. Grade A.

Hotel Lito (tel: 23511/23512). This modern, 97-room hotel, located in the centre of Ixós opposite a stretch of shingle beach, is a particular favourite with British visitors. Facilities include a freshwater swimming pool surrounded by extensive sun-bathing terraces, an attractive restaurant, and a lively bar. Disadvantages include the fact that some rooms are subject to noise from an adjacent taverna, and some of the sea-view bedrooms suffer from traffic noise. The three-sided lifts used here have warning signs and emergency buttons. Grade B.
Hotel Metropolitan Capsis (tel: 25015/25). An impressive, well-designed hotel surrounded by spacious gardens and sunny terraces, the 693-room Metropolitan Capsis offers a choice of lounges, bars, a card room, hairdresser's, shops, two swimming pools, a terrace snack bar and a taverna. There is also a children's playground and a well-equipped nursery for toddlers under the age of six. Dancing is a regular feature in the hotel's 'Roof Garden' discothèque, and an extensive entertainments programme includes fashion shows, games, Greek evenings and video shows. For the active there are two tennis courts, a games room with table tennis and billiards, aerobics, and basketball and volleyball courts. Grade A.
Miramare Beach (tel: 24251). This is a complex of luxury bungalows, all with sea views, set amid well-tended gardens packed with trees, and situated close to a 1,000-yard/metre long stretch of beach. The hotel's restaurant is noted for its cuisine, and there is a pleasant piano bar situated next to the swimming pool. Deluxe.
Oceanis Hotel (tel: 24881). This well-located hotel enjoys an excellent reputation for its cuisine, both international and Greek. Situated across the busy coast road from a stretch of shingle beach, it is within ten minutes' walk of the centre of Ixós, and three miles (5km) from Rhodes Town. Recently refurbished, it offers a medium-sized seawater swimming pool, spacious public areas and, for children, high chairs, early meals and children's menus. Guests with youngsters should note that the swimming pool carries no depth markings. Grade A.
Hotel Olympic Palace (tel: 28755). The hotel offers an impressive range of amenities and facilities for visitors of all ages. Situated opposite its own private, gently sloping sand-and-pebble beach – reached across the busy main road – it has an outdoor swimming pool set in well-equipped sun terraces and pretty gardens; an indoor swimming pool; poolside snack bar; spacious lounges; card and television rooms; a women's hairdressing salon; and various shops. For children there is a paddling pool, playground, cots, high chairs, babysitting, and early dinners on request. Meals in the hotel's main restaurant offer a choice of international dishes, with waiter service for both lunch and dinner. The **Aegean** nightclub features a disco most evenings as well as

regular Greek evenings. Live entertainment is provided regularly in the main bar. Sports facilities include a tennis court, mini-golf, games room with table tennis and video games, a gymnasium, and bicycle rental. Although it is officially classified as deluxe, standards have tended to decline slightly in recent years.

Rhodes Imperial Hotel (tel: 75000). A modern complex, built in 1993, nestling against the green hillside by the bay of Ixiá. One of the most luxurious hotels on the island with superb leisure facilities, including three swimming pools, tennis and squash courts and fully equipped gym. Other features include a ballroom, hairdresser and a daily entertainment programme as well as a safe private beach. Deluxe.

Rodos Bay Hotel (tel: 23661). Beautifully tucked into the side of pine-covered hills, the Rodos Bay offers stunning views from its top floor/terraces. Ixós beach is reached via a tunnel under the main road, and the centre of the resort is a 20-minute walk away. The hotel's rooftop outdoor swimming pool has a poolside bar for drinks and snacks. Other amenities include gardens, shops, a hairdressing salon, television/video room, lounges, restaurant, two bars and a sauna. Barbecues featuring Greek dancing are held regularly, as are live music sessions in the taverna. There is also a nightclub, tennis court and table tennis facilities. Children have their own separate freshwater pool. Grade A.

Rodos Palace Hotel and Apartments (tel: 25222). The Rodos Palace is a tall building facing out over the beach and sea. The complex consists of a large, modern luxury hotel and

Relaxing by the Rodos Palace pool

blocks of apartments, studios and bungalows dotted among the gardens. During the day, as an alternative to the beach, guests can relax around the spacious indoor and outdoor swimming pools. The hotel offers a selection of restaurants, bars, lounges and shops, a sauna, hairdressing salon and, for sports enthusiasts, table tennis, mini-golf, three tennis courts, crazy-golf, volleyball, waterpolo and a games room with electronic games. Entrance to the hotel's **Club Tropicana** discothèque is free. Children's needs are well catered for, with a pool of their own and a playground. Early suppers can be served in bedrooms, and cots and high chairs are available. Deluxe.

Restaurants and Entertainment
There are few restaurants in Ixós offering genuine Greek food, most specialising in foreign dishes such as smorgasbord, burgers, pizzas and spaghetti. A varied selection of international and Greek dishes, however, is offered at the **Sea House** pub/restaurant, right on the beach. Nightlife in Ixós is plentiful. Restaurants and tavernas that line the main coastal road bustle with activity, and many – such as the **Delfinia** – even have live music. Ixós is also the site of one of Rhodes' most popular discothèques, **Sodoma**. Though pricey, the light show is sophisticated and the music up-to-the-minute. At the **Mercedes PlayBoy** disco, you will find one of the most talented disc jockeys on the island.

Shopping
Ixos has a reasonable selection of mini-markets selling basic holiday needs such as sunscreen, film, soft drinks and supplies for self-catering holiday-makers, but a much wider selection is available in Rhodes Town, easily reached by bus or taxi.

◆◆◆ KAMEÍROS ✓

northwest coast, about 21 miles (34km) from Rhodes Town
Kameíros (sometimes spelled Kamiros) is one of the three ancient cities of Rhodes, and well worth visiting, not least for its delightful position. Abandoned at about the time of Christ, it is one of the best preserved of Classical Greek towns, with houses rising each side of a central street leading upwards from a newly excavated area, mainly of 3rd-century BC buildings.
Built on successively ascending terraces on a fertile hill, it is believed that the site was inhabited from the prehistoric period. Evidence indicates it flourished before the island's colonisation by the Dorians, although, it did not attain the prominence of its sister towns of Líndos and Ialyssós.
However, it continued to be inhabited until the 4th century AD, when it appears to have been mysteriously abandoned.

Long Buried
Kameíros was rediscovered in 1859 by Salzmann and Biliotti who carried out extensive excavations, uncovering a cemetery which yielded numerous finds now on display in the British Museum in London. These include a small terracotta basket of fruit, a metal cup containing hen's eggs, and a terracotta figure of a woman kneading dough. Much more major excavation work was carried out after 1929 by Italian archaeologists, whose work was interrupted by the war.

The ancient city of Kameíros

What to See

In its heyday the city spread out over a valley, with the unfortified acropolis on the highest point to the south. On the acropolis, which is approximately 400 feet (120m) above sea-level, were found archaic statues now on display in the Museum of Rhodes (Mouseío Archaiologikó) in Rhodes Town. Here, too, stood a Temple of Athena Polias, of which only the foundations remain. The temple was built in the 6th or 5th century BC, then restored and added to later on during the Hellenistic period (3rd–2nd centuries BC).

In front was a 650-foot (200m) long Doric stoa, or walkway, six columns of which were restored by the Italians but have since toppled over. An enormous cistern (6th-century BC) can be seen outside the stoa. A narrow path ran along most of the length of this, and beyond here was the public area of the market square.

The area of the city occupied by private houses, which has already been excavated, spreads out to the north of the acropolis, although it represents only part of the total area. Some of the houses are reasonably well preserved, and feature interior courtyards surrounded by a colonnade. Most private houses are from the Hellenistic period.

Several travel agents organise excursions to Kameíros, which can also be reached by bus from Mandraki Harbour, Rhodes Town.

Open: daily 08.30–17.00hrs.
Closed: Mondays.

◆◆◆

KAMEÍROS SKÁLA

About 10 miles (16km) to the south of the ancient city is Kameíros Skála, once the busy harbour for the inland town of Kritiniá, originally a Cretan settlement. Today it is a delightful, sleepy little harbour complete with colourful fishing boats and a couple of bar-restaurants specialising, not surprisingly, in fish. The best is probably **Althemenis**, which has a delightful terrace bordering the sea.

In the high season summer months a boat takes passengers through a group of offshore islands to **Chálki** (see page opposite), whose harbour and pleasant seaside capital are understandably beginning to attract visitors from Rhodes.

Close to Kameíros Skála is **Kástellos**, an impressive ruined fortress, built by the Knights of St John, and reached by a loop off the main road. The Knights were attracted by the site's strategic position commanding nearly 50 miles (80km) of the western coastline, and they built the castle on a grand scale. The fortress is worth visiting for the views alone – not only of the coastline and sea, but even landward, where Mount Atáviros dominates.

◆◆

KATTAVÍA

about 60 miles (96km) south of Rhodes Town

This small village, almost at the southern tip of Rhodes, consists of a couple of shops and a few tavernas with a pleasant local atmosphere, especially in the

evenings. The village church is noted for its frescoes. The magnificent beach at nearby **Prasonísi** is reached by a five-mile (8km) track, creating an isthmus connecting the mainland with the 'island' of Prasonísi, or Leak Island. This beach is excellent for windsurfing, but there are no organised facilities apart from a small but usually lively taverna. The nearby beaches at **Apolakkiá** and **Monólithos** provide good seclusion at any time of the year, and the surrounding countryside offers plenty of interest for walkers.

Painted icon of the Virgin and Child in the village church at Kattavía

◆◆◆
CHÁLKI
off the northwest coast of Rhodes
Chálki is a mountainous little island, the sort of place you could either love or hate. It offers a quiet, relaxing style of life with absolutely nothing to do except stroll across a rather barren landscape to a good sandy beach or a number of sandy coves; explore a ruined village, from where there are good views of Rhodes and other nearby islands; or eat at one of

the small selection of tavernas along the attractive harbourside. Here you can get to know some of the locals who, through years of emigration, now have strong family ties in many parts of the world, especially America and Australia.

Niborio, the chief village, is sited round the harbour. Although there are no hotels, accommodation is available in private houses and there are bungalows by the sea. The nearest beach is Pandemos Beach, a ten-minute walk on the other side of the hill behind the town.

Chora, 2½ miles (4km) from Niborio, was a flourishing centre in the 18th and 19th centuries but the hilltop town is now practically deserted. The medieval castle with the ruins of a church behind it offers a magnificent view from its location above the village.

If you decide to stay on the island you should be prepared to put up with the very real probability of interruptions to the local fresh water supplies, as Chálki relies almost totally on water being delivered by boat from the mainland. But if you can cope with this, you should find the island ideal for a week or a few days' relaxation away from it all.

The boat trip to Chálki from Kameíros Skála on the west coast of Rhodes takes one and a half hours, with daily sailings scheduled at 15.00hrs. However, times vary at the discretion of the boat owners, so it is wise to check in advance. Cost of the journey is negotiable with the boat owners.

◆◆

CHARÁKI

east coast

The fishing village and resort of Charáki is built round an attractive crescent-shaped bay, with a fine shingle-and-sand beach offering crystal-clear swimming and excellent snorkelling. It has been a popular lunchtime, weekend and holiday spot with Greeks for some time, so tavernas in the bay offer excellent fish. **Argo's** is probably the best, though it is not cheap. Visitors can enjoy watching the fish being unloaded from the colourful caïques as they return from night fishing trips in the early mornings.

The village is overlooked by ruined **Feráklos Castle**, occupying an extensive flat area on a hilltop. The castle was built by the Knights of St John and was one of their most powerful fortresses. It was used as a jailhouse for both war and civil prisoners, and was one of the last castles on the island to fall to the invading Turks in the 16th century. To the north are the remains of ancient tombs and a church which is decorated with frescoes of the 15th and 17th centuries. A road runs through orange and lemon groves to the village of **Másari**, about one and a half miles (2.5km) away, while the superb sandy bay of **Agathi**, one of the island's best, is a 25-minute walk to the north.

Accommodation

Accommodation in Charáki is in self-catering rooms and apartments.

Fishing boat moored in Kolýmpia cove

◆◆
KOLÝMPIA
east coast

A long shady avenue of eucalyptus trees, lined by a handful of *pensions* and tavernas, leads down from the busy main Rhodes Town–Líndos road to Kolýmpia's sand-and-shingle beach. Here you will find several tavernas and bars, watersports, sunbeds and umbrellas. Near by is a smaller cove with fishing boats and a taverna as well as a tiny fishing harbour. At present Kolýmpia is a relatively unspoiled and charming spot – even if the beach itself is somewhat ordinary – but a considerable amount of building work is taking place, designed to transform it into one of the island's major resorts.

At the heart of the village is a large square containing homes for the aged. To the left a road runs about two miles (3km) through the avenue of eucalyptus trees down to the sea. Along this road, in a peach grove, lie the remains of a 6th-century AD basilica and some mosaic flooring, hidden among grasses and with walls no more than three feet (1m) high. Continuing along the road, you reach a fork. The path to the right takes you to a fine sandy beach below a rise; the left fork leads to a small cove with a jetty, a restaurant, and a long sand-and-shingle beach particularly suitable for children because of the shallowness of the water near the shore. Waterskis, windsurfers and pedaloes can all be rented and are generally in good condition. Kolýmpia enjoys easy access to Faliráki, Rhodes Town and Líndos, while the airport is about 25 miles (40km) away.

Accommodation

Irene Palace (tel: 56263). Situated in a quiet area close to Kolýmpia, this is a well-maintained, family-run hotel offering 188 rooms, most with a terrace and all with private facilities. Cots and baby-sitting are available on request. There is a large freshwater swimming pool surrounded by gardens and lawns and a separate children's pool as well as a children's playground on a grassy surface. Exterior public areas are spacious and relaxing, and the hotel staff friendly and helpful. Buffet breakfasts and lunches are served in the snack bar, and dinner is also a buffet, with four courses. Early meals and children's menus are available on request.

Entertainment consists of organised games, a Happy Hour, bingo, and party evenings. Grade A.

Apart from this hotel, other holiday accommodation is available in small, unpretentious hotels or numerous studios and apartments.

Restaurants

The choice of restaurants and bars in Kolýmpia is limited. The best of those that do exist is probably the beachside **Nissaki**, which has a shady, vine-covered terrace and another terrace bordering the sea.

◆◆

KREMASTÍ

west coast, about 8 miles (13km) from Rhodes Town

The blossoming resort of Kremastí centres round the main street, lined by tavernas, small shops and cafés – the kind of place where you can still get a real village *souvláki* (kebab). The wide pebbly beach is about 10 minutes' walk from the centre of the resort, and there is a bus service to Rhodes Town and to the lively resort of Ixós, only 4 miles (6.5km) away.

The church of Our Lady of Kremastí

What to See
The unusual modern church of Our Lady of Kremastí was built not *on* the site of a former church but, strangely, *around* it. The interior is worth inspecting for the pretty side chapel. Also in the village is a large modern church decorated in the Byzantine style which was paid for by villagers who had emigrated to the US. The interior is very richly decorated.
In the necropolis around Kremastí were found several examples of Geometric and Archaic vases which are now on display in the Archaeological Museum in Rhodes Town.

August Festivities
The villagers of Kremastí celebrate in ancient style the festival of the **Assumption of the Virgin**, an important festival in Greece. The actual date is 15 August, but the celebrations last from 14 to 23 August, including a large-scale flea-market, fiesta and funfare.

Accommodation
Most accommodation in Kremastí is in blocks of self-catering apartments. These include the huge **Filérimos** complex, (tel: 92933) which has almost 100 bungalows in landscaped grounds plus around the same number of apartments. Class A.

Restaurants
The **International** bar/restaurant is popular with late-night revellers, while nearby **Mike's** snack bar/cafeteria offers a good selection of dishes – though the music tends to be on the loud side!

◆◆◆
LÁRDOS
southeast coast
Lárdos is an attractive, small but developing village popular with those looking for the chance to unwind and sample Greek life. In the colourful village square there is a fountain of spa water, a reasonable choice of shops for those catering for themselves, and a variety of reasonably priced tavernas. The imposing Italian architecture here is a legacy of Mussolini's day. From the village you can embark on one of a series of lovely walks through olive and lemon groves to places such as **Pefka** with its attractive sand-and-shingle beach and tavernas. One of the island's two campsites is located at Lárdos, and the bay below has miles of shingle and sand-dunes.

Restaurants and Entertainment
You can get a plate of delicious mixed seafood at **Maria's Restaurant**, in the main square, while nearby **Roula's Taverna** specialises in grilled dishes of pork, lamb and chicken as well as hamburgers. **Memories** cocktail bar has a good selection of drinks, a smart terrace with palm trees and plants, and a lovely roof garden.

◆◆
MONÍ THÁRI (THARI MONASTERY)
southeast Rhodes
Remotely situated 2½ miles (4km) from the village of Láerma, the monastery is, in fact, a small, domed church set in a clearing in the woods. Though it is neglected and solitary, a visit here is recommended, not least for the

Moní Thári
According to legend, Thári was founded by a Byzantine princess in thanks for the cure she obtained from the fresh woodland countryside. The north and south walls of the church contain 12th-century parts, but there are some 9th-century remains in the grounds surrounding it. Of greatest interest to visitors are the fine wall paintings. Some areas of the church carry as many as four layers of paintings, and these are dated to about 1100, 1200, 1500 and 1700. Those in the apse depict the hierarchy of apostles in tones of burnt red ochre, black and cream, and there is also a group of prophets. On the right wall is a head of a horse, possibly part of a painting of St George or St Demetrius.

monastery's magnificent frescoes. The broad courtyard with its numerous cells is testimony to the important role the monastery once played. It can be reached by turning inland off the main road at Lárdos (7½ miles/12km west of Líndos) towards Láerma. From there turn left, and follow a forest road to Thari.

◆◆
MONÓLITHOS
west coast
Monólithos – the name means 'one stone' – is the site of a ruined castle dramatically perched on an isolated hill-crest and offering visitors one of the best views on the island. Not a great deal of masonry survives from the fortress built by Grand Master d'Aubusson, apart from the remains of a small chapel beside which a modern church has been built. Goat bells resound across the valleys, and the castle overlooks the round islet of Strongýlo. The approach to the castle, along a stony track, is steep and hazardous, with a sheer drop down on the other side, but the resultant views are definitely worth the effort.

Monólithos castle perched on its rock

◆◆◆

PETALOÚDES (VALLEY OF THE BUTTERFLIES)

about 15 miles (25km) from Rhodes Town

A popular excursion spot, Petaloúdes (the word means 'butterflies') occupies an extensively foliaged site, steeply climbing, and complete with a pretty stream that tumbles in a series of rock pools and waterfalls. You can walk in the valley along a pathway which criss-crosses the stream and pools via rustic bridges and rock steps. Delightful though the scene is, it is not for this that hordes of tourists descend in the summer, but for the butterflies, which are a feature. The butterflies – which are in fact a species of tiger moth – are dark brown and cream when their wings are folded, and red, black, brown and white when in flight. They are attracted to the resin of the storax trees with which the valley abounds, and hundreds of thousands of them migrate to the valley to mate between June and the end of September each year. In recent times the numbers of butterflies have declined significantly, largely because sightseers have been frightening them into flight during the daytime (they are a nocturnal species) by clapping their hands or blowing whistles. This is now forbidden. (See also **Peace and Quiet** page 87.)

Open: daily 09.00–18.00hrs. Entrance fee. Car parking space is available.

Near Petaloúdes, and reached from the middle of the valley, where the buses stop, is the **Monastery of the Virgin Mary of Kalopetra** (Moní Kalopetra). This delightful church was built in 1782 by Alexander Ypsilantis, known as the grandfather of the Greek national uprising, and a visit is well worth the upward climb.

◆◆◆

PEFKA

east coast

If you ever wondered where families from Líndos go for a brief escape from the invading hordes of visitors in the summer, the answer is Pefka 3 miles (5km) away. Once a sleepy huddle of houses amid fig orchards and vineyards, the village has grown, but is still a popular hideaway that has not yet been spoiled by over-development. Pefka's popularity has grown in recent years and there has been much new building, but happily most of the new establishments are well-designed studio and apartment blocks which blend in well with the surroundings, rather than huge hotel complexes.

What particularly attracts about Pefka is its long sandy beach sloping gently into the sea – ideal for children. Dotted with numerous small, secluded bays, there are some rocks at either end of the main beach, providing access to good snorkelling as an alternative to lazing in the sun. During the more popular months, beds, umbrellas and windsurfing boards can be hired. There are several small mini-markets in the resort where self-caterers can find most of their basic requirements, and car, moped and motorbike rentals are readily available.

Accommodation

Hotel Thalia (tel: 44508). Opened in 1989, this smart, 68-room hotel is quietly situated some ten minutes' walk from the beach. Amenities provided include a swimming pool, small bar with large sun terrace, and breakfast room. All rooms have shower and a balcony or terrace. Grade C.

Other accommodation available is comprised of self-catering apartments and studios.

Restaurants and Entertainment

There are several good tavernas with varied menus – from fresh fish and *kalamari* to *spaghetti carbonara*. There are also half a dozen popular bars and a discothèque for revellers, sensibly soundproofed. This can be lively or quiet, depending on the season, but for swinging nightlife Líndos is only a taxi ride or an hour's walk away.

The **Greek House** restaurant, near the beach, specialises not surprisingly in Greek dishes including grilled and barbecued meat and fish. The **Kelari** bar has a pleasant, shady terrace, and the **Peacock** bar a roof terrace with commanding views over the bay.

◆◆◆

PROFÍTIS ILÍAS

northwest Rhodes

A winding, wooded, mountain road leads from the village of Sálakos – noted for its gardens and flowers – to the heights of Mount Profítis Ilías. Profítis Ilías is the name usually given to the highest summit on any Greek island because the prophet Elias ascended to heaven from a mountain top. On Rhodes, however, the highest summit is Attávyros, which is associated with Zeus. It is possible to drive nearly to the top of the 4,000-foot (1,215m) high peak of the mountain, which is heavily wooded and somewhat reminiscent of the lower Alps.

Situated on the eastern and lower slopes of the mountain, the church of Ágios Nikólaos Fountoúkli is worth visiting for the excellent frescoes of the 14th and 15th centuries which cover the interior and which, together with the building itself, were endowed by an administrative official whose three children had died as a result of the plague. This is why the church was dedicated to St Nicholas, the protector of children. Though some of the frescoes have been overpainted and touched up, they are still striking. Of particular note is one depicting St Michael bearing a huge sword, and another of a man (the donor), his wife and his three children, upholding between them the church of Christ – and the Church of St Nicholas.

Accommodation

Elafos-Elfina (tel: 22231). This chalet-style building at the summit of the pine-clad peak would not look out of place in Switzerland. It seems to have been inspired by the surrounding forests of pungent pines. The hotel/lodge is an excellent choice for those who enjoy country settings rather than beach resorts, though it opens for only a very limited period in the peak summer months. The views from here across the west coast are splendid, and in spring the woods are carpeted in anemones and cyclamen. The hotel is operated by the Astir group (which also runs the deluxe Grand Hotel Astir Palace in Rhodes Town). Grade A.

Ágios Nikólaos Fountoúkli church is renowned for its frescoes

◆◆◆
SÝMI
about 15 miles (24km) north of Rhodes island

The small, friendly island of Sými, which lies between two Turkish peninsulas, is an increasingly popular place for an interesting day's excursion from Rhodes – it is the second nearest of the Dodecanese after Chálki. It is also becoming more popular as a holiday destination in its own right, although a shortage of accommodation is a problem many would-be visitors encounter. At first sight the island appears unoccupied and barren, apart from a few pine forests; but as you approach the long harbour you discover a large, 19th-century Greek island town, preserved in almost perfect detail. The little port of **Gialós** is breathtaking, with typical Dodecanese mansions in ochre and pastel shades in tiers on the rocky hillsides. Many were abandoned or bombed in World War II, but they are now being restored from their state of faded glory. A row of windmills stands on the ridge above the harbour and several of these have been restored as holiday homes, most owned by German and Swiss visitors. Fresh water supplies for washing can be a problem on Sými, and in the high season you should be prepared for occasional water rationing. The village is also steeply stepped, making it unsuitable for the elderly or those with walking difficulties. As an example, there are about 500 steps from the

harbour to the museum in the upper town, and 650 steps to the very top of the town. Those seeking a relaxing, peaceful holiday should also be warned that between the hours of 11.00 and 16.00 the port becomes very crowded with day trippers from Rhodes.

The harbour area is the social centre of the island, where most of the shops, tavernas and cafés are located. Down on the other side of Chorió – the upper village – a road leads through a valley to **Pédio**, a hamlet of fishermen's cottages, which now has a hotel on the sandy shore, several tavernas, and an 'ouzeri' where you can sample a Nun's Bikini cocktail made from the unusual local cactus flower liqueur!

Sými is especially attractive at Easter, when special cheese pies and biscuits are baked. On Easter Saturday night fireworks fill the air in celebration of the great festival.

What to See and Do

Motorcycles can be hired for sightseeing, but there is only one stretch of tarred road, linking Pédio and Gialós with the island's famous monastery. However, the island now boasts an air-conditioned coach to take you in style through the interior to **Moní (Monastery of) Taxíarchis Michael** at Panormítis – a vast, white edifice in a lovely horseshoe bay and a place of pilgrimage for Greeks worldwide. The Archangel Michael is the island's patron saint and protector of sailors. The church is rich with gold and silver offerings from grateful mariners, and there is a small museum in the peaceful courtyard. Sometimes there is a stop at another small monastery on the way, and you can return by boat after relaxing on the beach at Marathoúnta.

Daily excursions are available by caïque to various bays around the island, all offering sheltered shingle or pebble beaches, with excellent swimming and snorkelling in crystal-clear waters.

If you are interested in walking, apart from the endless exploration of the town and nearby fertile valley, there are guided walks in summer over the island by a resident Englishman. They start at about 07.00hrs to escape the main heat of the sun, and last two to five hours, depending on the route, with various stops for rest and looking at the interesting aspects of the island. These walks normally finish by joining up with an excursion boat for a barbecue lunch.

The pretty harbour town of Gialós, on Sými, is half deserted

Accommodation

Accommodation on Sými is expensive and difficult to obtain, especially if you are looking for a single night's stay – owners usually insist on a minimum of two or three days' room occupation. The general standard of accommodation is fairly basic.

Hotel Aliki, Gialós (tel: 71665). Arguably the best hotel on the island, this large, neoclassical mansion, situated on the sea front, has been tastefully converted to a small hotel, with 15 rooms of varying sizes, furnished to a high standard. On the ground floor there is an elegant bar and breakfast room, and there is also a roof-garden with magnificent views of the bay of Sými. It is possible to swim and snorkel off the rocks directly in front of the hotel, and it is only five minutes' walk to the central harbour area. The owner provides a warm and welcoming atmosphere. Grade A.

Chorio Hotel, Chorió (tel: 71800). This recently-built bed-and-breakfast hotel is situated at the end of the row of windmills above the port. The hotel is in true Sými style, only two storeys high and painted a wonderful sky blue. The rooms have been well furnished, with great attention to detail. Nine have private balconies, and there are several quiet terraces and patios where guests can sit and enjoy peace, sunshine and a drink from the bar. There is also a comfortable lounge and a pretty dining room. The hotel is only five minutes away from Chorió's lively tavernas, and right next to the village bus stop, with buses going to both Pédio Bay and the harbour area. Grade B.

Hotel Grace, Gialós (tel: 71415). This small, family-run bed-and-breakfast hotel is situated in a quiet position about five minutes' walk from Gialós' tavernas and shops. Yiannis, the owner, has recently added a new wing, with three rooms and two studios, all of which share a beautiful terrace with glorious views over the harbour. The rooms all have refrigerators and private bathrooms with solar water heating. There is a telephone in reception for guests' use, and breakfast is served under a leafy vine on the terrace. The rooms are all nicely furnished, and the hotel has been built to a very high standard. Grade B.

Kokona Hotel, Gialós (tel: 71451). This spotless, family-run bed-and-breakfast hotel stands on the harbour level, two minutes' walk from the quayside yet in one of the quietest spots in Sými's harbour village. Fotis, the owner, is a carpenter by trade, and his skills are apparent in the attractive bedrooms, with lovely pinewood fixtures and furnishings. Each room has a telephone, fan, and private bathroom with hot water. Most have either balcony or terrace. Kokona, Fotis' wife, serves breakfast on the vine-covered terrace outside the hotel, and in the basement there is a small bar. Grade B.

Pedi Beach Hotel, Pédio (tel: 71276). The hotel is situated at Pédio Beach, about 40 minutes' walk from Sými harbour. All the rooms have balconies or terraces, and most face the sea. The situation is quiet, with a beautiful outlook over the countryside or the sea. A regular bus service or a short journey by taxi takes you to either Chorió or Sými harbour, for a wider choice of restaurants, bars and shopping. Grade B.

Restaurants and Entertainment

For eating out, there are many tavernas around the harbour-front, and also in the upper town of Chorió: fresh fish and locally caught shrimps are a speciality. At weekends there are usually impromptu bouzouki evenings in Chorió and Pédio, but every night the tavernas, cafés and bars can become quite lively. Well away from the port are two discothèques.

Fishermen's chapel at Stégna

◆◆
STÉGNA
east coast

Though not exactly the prettiest resort on Rhodes, Stégna is certainly one of the least spoiled and least commercialised, as yet virtually undiscovered by the masses. Set on the side of an attractive bay, the village straggles along the seashore, and includes several fishermen's shacks and a couple of unpretentious tavernas – an ideal spot for those who enjoy simple pleasures without any frills. As for the beach, there is a fine, shingle, sandy foreshore giving way to pebbles; although not really equipped for visitors, it does have a few beach umbrellas and windsurfing boards for hire, and there are also beach showers. The resort is reached from the village of Archángelos via a winding, tortuous road complete with hairpin bends, so care needs to be taken, whether you are driving or on foot.

◆◆
THEOLÓGOS
west coast, about 14 miles (22km) from Rhodes Town

Though only three miles (5km) from the airport, Theológos remained an uncommercialised farming and fishing village longer than most. With only two large hotels and half a dozen smaller establishments, it remains one of Rhodes' less busy resorts, though its calm is shattered during high season by frequent aircraft noise. Theológos is still backed by fields and its pebble beach is rarely packed. There is a handful of tavernas, a mini-market and a baker's.

Accommodation

Hotel Doretta Beach (tel: 41440). This comfortable hotel has been a favourite with British visitors for many years. It stands in attractive gardens stretching down to the beach, about a mile (2km) from the village centre. The hotel is cool and spacious inside, and imaginative use of local stonework gives the décor a typical Greek quality. Facilities include a split-level lounge and bar, two lifts, a hairdresser, two shops, a supermarket, large swimming pool with sun terrace, poolside snack bar/taverna, and a children's club run by a supervisor. For toddlers there is also a paddling pool and a playground with a safe, sandy base; early dinners are available along with a special menu; and babysitting can be arranged on request. Grade A.

Hotel Meliton (tel: 41666). In a peaceful setting on the outskirts of Theológos – about 15 minutes' walk from shops and tavernas in the centre of the resort – the Meliton was built to a standard much higher than is normally expected of its C-grade rating. Facilities include a comfortable lounge bar and attractive gardens which contain a pool and tennis courts, with equipment available for hire.

Entertainment

The **Lemon Tree** bar along the road from the Hotel Doretta Beach is popular with visitors to the resort.

Mock-Oriental arch at the crumbling Italian-built spa at Kalithéa

◆◆◆
THÉRMES KALITHÉA (KALITHEA)

about 2½ miles (4km) south of Rhodes Town

Thérmes Kalithéa was built in the 1920s by the Italians as a spa. It enjoyed considerable popularity with visitors anxious to take what they believed were the healing waters, said to be beneficial in the treatment of rheumatism, arthritis, diabetes and kidney diseases. Now the attractive domed pavilions with pink marbled pillars and Moorish archways stand abandoned. But although its life as a health spa is over, Kalithea has a new lease of life as a holiday resort catering to sun-worshippers, with a small development growing up around the nearby small, sheltered cove. Here you will find a few tavernas and a small but pleasant shingle beach, with rocky coves. There is also a lido beneath the palm trees with sun-loungers and a café, and Kalithea also has the island's only dive centre.

Accommodation

Eden Roc Hotel (tel: 23851). Located along the bay of Kalithea, in the direction of Fáliraki, the Eden Roc fronts a rocky stretch of beach. It offers waterskiing, bicycling, windsurfing, two large tennis courts, and a sauna. Grade A.

Paradise Hotel (tel: 29220). One of Rhodes' finest hotels of its class, with a high standard of comfort and excellent facilities, the 645-room Paradise enjoys an attractive setting near Kalithea, with steps leading down from the sun terrace to the sheltered sand-and-shingle cove below. Among its amenities are a large swimming pool with sun terraces and gardens, together with beach and poolside bars; air-conditioning throughout in high season; two bars and lounges; discothèque and nightclub; and facilities for tennis, windsurfing, waterskiing, table tennis and mini-golf. For youngsters there is a children's pool, early suppers, and high chairs and cots on request. Grade A.

Sunwing Hotel (tel: 28600). Facilities here range from a large restaurant overlooking the swimming pool and sea to a beach taverna, cocktail bar, and grill terrace with dancing, shows and entertainment. Sports facilities include two tennis courts, mini-golf and volleyball. Grade A.

Restaurant

Home-made Greek dishes are a speciality of the restaurant/bar **Koskinou House**.

◆◆
TRIÁNTA

west coast

Triánta (or sometimes Trianda in tour operators' brochures) is rapidly developing as a resort, not least because of its convenient location not far from Rhodes Town and because it is on the doorstep of one of the most fascinating ancient sites on the island – Ialyssós. The resort is situated on the main route into Rhodes Town from the airport. The fact that it is quite close to the airport means that it suffers from occasional aircraft noise. Other disadvantages are that the sea here tends to be less calm than at other resorts along this coast, and that the beaches tend to shelve quite steeply, making it not the best choice for those with young children. That said, the grey sand-and-shingle beach – about fifteen minutes' walk from the resort centre – is very popular in the high season, especially with windsurfers and sailors. Pedaloes are available for rent and some of the hotels offer sports facilities.

First settled by Minoans from Crete in the 16th century BC, Triánta was inundated by tidal waves during the following century when the volcanic island of Santorini, near Crete, erupted. Today's visitors can enjoy a resort that retains a fair degree of village atmosphere, with a pleasant square containing bars, tavernas and cafés that are popular gathering places for visitors and locals.

Three or More?
Some say Triánta's name, which can be translated as 'thirty', derives from the establishment here of that number of summer villas belonging to the Knights of St John. A more likely explanation, though, is that the name started out as Triada or Aghia Triada (Holy Trinity) from a now-vanished church.

If you decide to venture away from the beach for a while you can explore the site of the ancient city of **Ialyssós**, with its 3rd-century temple, ruined castle, restored monastery and centuries-old Doric fountain (page 55). The church in Triánta, dedicated to the Assumption of the Holy Mary, has a splendidly carved 18th-century screen.

Accommodation
Accommodation in Triánta is mixed, with hotels of varying standards and also self-catering apartments and studios. The accommodation tends to be spread out over quite an extensive area, with some establishments in isolated positions away from the village.

Blue Horizon Hotel (tel: 93484). A recently built hotel with 221 rooms, bungalows and suites, each with terrace or balcony, bathroom, telephone and radio, the Blue Horizon is located on a stretch of shingle beach about ten minutes from the resort centre. The hotel's reception area is attractively designed and filled with tropical plants, and there is a large, pleasant dining room, snack bar, swimming pool, children's pool and playground, bar and taverna. Grade A.

Filérimos Hotel (tel: 29510). Located about ten minutes' walk from the beach and 15 minutes from the centre of Triánta, the Filérimos is part of a complex that also includes apartment accommodation. Facilities, shared by all guests, include two swimming pools set in sun terraces, a poolside snack bar, two lounges, a supermarket and a gift shop. The hotel's taverna offers a choice of local and international dishes, while regular Greek evenings are a popular feature, as is dancing to records in one of the hotel's lounge bars. Grade A.

Hotel Golden Beach (tel: 92411). Superbly located on a private stretch of pebble beach, with

Doric temple ruins, Ialyssós

views of the sea from the front and of mountains from the rear, the Golden Beach is a pleasant, well-maintained hotel that is popular with families and fully justifies its A-grade classification. There are 196 twin-bedded rooms and 10 singles, all with air-conditioning, balconies and private facilities, and there are also 55 self-catering apartments. The Olympic-sized swimming pool is complemented by a separate, freshwater children's pool; both are set in attractive gardens. There is also a restaurant, a snack bar, a piano bar and a nightclub offering open-air dancing.

Hotel Sunflower (tel: 93893). Popular with German, Dutch and English visitors, this is an impressive 87-room hotel that offers a large, oblong swimming pool and beautiful gardens with plenty of sunbeds, tables and chairs.

The small dining room offers an international menu, with buffet breakfasts, and there are early meals for children. On the negative side, there is a potentially dangerous three-sided lift, and no depth marking in the swimming pool, making careful supervision of children necessary. Grade A.

Restaurants and Entertainment

For evening entertainment there are several local restaurants serving Greek cuisine and there is also a popular disco for the young-at-heart. One of the most unusual café/bars is created from an old windmill sitting right by the beach and called, not surprisingly, the **Windmill**. The nearby **Trata** taverna specialises in fresh fish.

◆◆

TSAMPÍKA

east coast, about 18 miles (30km) from Rhodes Town

This is a beautiful bay bordered by a long, sandy beach, approached down a steep access road. Some guide books describe the place as being uncrowded and undiscovered, but in fact it is extremely popular in high summer, attracting people staying in other parts of the island, who come here in their droves by coach, rented cars and even boats. Beach and watersports lovers, however, are well catered for, with rafts, pedaloes, speedboats, umbrellas and sunbeds all available for rent, and the adventurous can even try parascending here. **Vidal's Saloon**, a small but popular beach taverna, has a shower point on the edge of its patio. Away from the beach, a turning off the Tsampíka Beach road leads to a white, Byzantine monastery surrounded by stone walls. Being set close to the mountain top, it affords splendid views. On 8 September each year, women wishing to conceive climb the steep approach on foot and pray that they may give birth.

◆◆◆

GENNÁDIO (GENNADI)

southeast coast

On such a popular island as Rhodes, it is surprising that until

Orange trees – a refreshing sight

quite recently Gennádio has escaped the attention of most holiday companies, although this is changing rapidly, with studios and apartments beginning to spring up. The village is surrounded by delightful countryside and some of the best beaches on the island, though Gennádio beach itself is of sand and shingle. Numerous tracks lead down from the road to the beach, with its dunes and crystal-clear sea, and also to numerous seafood tavernas found on this pretty coastline. The nightlife is limited to a handful of cocktail bars and a single disco; but for those opting for self-catering accommodation, there are a few mini-markets, and a post office.

PEACE AND QUIET
Wildlife and Countryside on Rhodes
by Paul Sterry

Although it is extremely popular as a tourist destination, most of the associated development on Rhodes has been concentrated in a few areas, largely along the coast and in the north of the island. Happily, much of the interior and southern half remains unspoiled.

For such a comparatively small island, Rhodes boasts a wide range of habitats. The coastline is superb, with dramatic cliffs, isolated coves and deserted and windswept beaches. Inland there are still areas of natural woodland, sadly depleted by recent fires, together with maquis and *phrygana* vegetation – habitats typical of many Mediterranean islands. Much of the remaining land is under cultivation, but because the farming is not intensive, the small fields still support a surprising range of wildlife.

Although there is wildlife interest throughout the year, spring is undoubtedly the best season to visit Rhodes. Migrant birds are newly arrived and flowers bloom everywhere.

The Coast

The seas and coast which surround Rhodes are perhaps its crowning glory: there are stunning sea cliffs and beautiful sandy beaches, many of which – especially on the west coast – are virtually deserted. The seas are full of marine life – food for a typical range of Mediterranean seabirds – while on land, the coast is home to colourful maritime plants.

The west coast of Rhodes in particular is constantly buffeted by onshore winds and consequently is noticeably cooler than the east side of the island. From about 11.00hrs onwards the winds pick up and oceanic birds such as Cory's shearwaters and Mediterranean shearwaters often pass surprisingly close to shore. Both species are masters of the air and their gliding flight, on outstretched wings, is seemingly effortless. They fly in long lines of birds, close to the water, and characteristically twist and turn to make the most of the sea breezes.

Snorkelling in the clear, blue waters reveals a wealth of life unseen from land. Because the Mediterranean has an extremely small tidal range, rock pools are seldom exposed, and marine creatures such as sea urchins, starfish and sea anemones have to be viewed from under water.

Some marine life does get washed ashore after strong winds, however, and sea balls – compacted balls of sea grass – are often conspicuous. For those who do not wish to go snorkelling or scuba diving, there is an excellent marine aquarium in Rhodes Town.

The flowers of the coast are at their best in spring and early summer. Along the cliffs, look for hottentot fig – an introduction from southern Africa – while shingle beaches and sand dunes may have species such as yellow-horned

A bee-eater surveys the scene

poppy and purple spurge, together with the ubiquitous agave or century plant. When in flower, the plants of the sand dunes are visited by colourful butterflies, including clouded yellows and painted ladies, as well as day-flying hummingbird hawk moths.

Agricultural Land

The farming methods on Rhodes are generally traditional and small scale, and the landscape has probably changed little over the last hundred years. Small fields, surrounded by stone walls built from rubble removed from the soil, are typical, as are olive groves and orchards of citrus fruits. The tall spires of funereal cypress trees dot the landscape and a surprising range of wildlife flourishes alongside the crops.

One of the pleasures of walking on Rhodes is the delightful small fields, full of colourful flowers in spring. A wide range of arable 'weeds' can be found among the cereal crops and more especially in fallow fields. Star thistles – plants with typical thistle flowers but incredibly spiny stems and leaves – grape hyacinths, anemones and poppies appear, and even in the height of summer, field eryngo – another very spiny plant – St John's worts, mulleins and mallows can be found. The flowers are visited by butterflies such as the elegant scarce swallowtail, while on the ground, grasshoppers and crickets scurry for cover.

Farm buildings and overgrown gardens sometimes harbour interesting birds and insects. The sound of cicadas is deafening during the height of summer, many of their number falling victim to praying mantids which lurk among the foliage. Serins – wild relatives of the canary – are less intrusive, singing their jingling song from the tops of trees.

Maquis

Originally, much of Rhodes would have been cloaked in evergreen oaks and pines, with a rich understorey of flowers appearing in glades and rides. Over the centuries, the trees were gradually cleared for timber, firewood and to create agricultural land. In many areas, the forests never fully regenerated, partly due to the actions of grazing animals. However, a form of natural vegetation – maquis – colonised some areas, characterised by a wide range of colourful and aromatic plants.

On Rhodes, maquis vegetation

is typical of many of the mountain roads, such as that between Afántou (on the east coast) and Psínthos. Kermes oak, whose leaves resemble miniature holly leaves, and mastic trees are prominent and there is usually a dense understorey of tree heathers, cistuses, rosemary, juniper, rock roses and thorn of Christ.

Many of the plants are spiny or have leaves which are waxy or aromatic; this discourages grazing animals and helps reduce water loss.

During the long, dry summer many Mediterranean snails go into a dormant state known as aestivation. They gather together in clusters, sometimes of several dozen individuals, on plant stems. The egg cases of praying mantids are also attached to stems and have an extremely hard texture.

Phrygana

Phrygana vegetation is typical of dry, stony land which in the past was probably covered by open, stunted woodland. This habitat is characterised by low-growing plants and shrubs, some of which are spiny and form dense, compact cushions. In addition to the more persistent species such as asphodels, hypericums, heathers and vetches, spring sees the appearance of grape hyacinths, French lavenders, spurges and cistuses.

One of the glories of a spring visit to Rhodes is the discovery of numerous orchids, both in *phrygana* and in maquis habitats. Several members of the bee orchid family are widespread. More showy in appearance are butterfly orchids, tongue orchids, bug orchids and giant orchids, the latter a particularly early flowering species. You are likely to come across them almost anywhere, but verges and abandoned fields can be particularly good. Orchids can be extraordinarily difficult to spot, even giant orchids, which regularly grow to three feet (one metre) tall, but once you have 'got your eye in' more and more will swim into view.

Birds of the Fields

Typical birds of agricultural land include crested larks, whose plumage blends in with the dusty soil. Look too for little owls perched on fence posts or overhanging branches. They will follow your movements with their eyes, and have the disconcerting ability to turn their heads almost through 180 degrees in any direction, including upside-down, without having to move their bodies. Corn buntings, whose song resembles jingling keys, are widespread and sing from exposed perches, while Sardinian warblers can be seen or heard wherever there is dense cover. In the summer, black-headed buntings perch on wires and branches.

In spring and autumn, migrant birds stop off to feed. Short-toed larks, black redstarts, tawny pipits and the occasional red-throated pipit can also be found feeding in bare fields. Birds of prey, including harriers and kestrels, quarter the fields in search of insects and small mammals, while bee-eaters and rollers perch on wires.

Forests and Mountains

With the exception of Mount Attávyros, most of the mountains on Rhodes are, to some extent, wooded. The forests comprise mainly pines, with some evergreen oaks, and often develop a rich understorey of maquis vegetation. Sadly, in recent years there have been extensive fires, many started deliberately, which have not only reduced the area of forests but also severely depleted the range of wildlife they support. Under the open canopy of many undisturbed pine woodlands, a dense layer of maquis plants such as tree heathers, junipers, cistuses and spurges can be found. The air is full of aromatic scents from the low-growing plants and the pines.

Mount Attávyros lies on the west side of Rhodes and rises to 4,000 feet (1,215m) above sea-level. A dramatic gorge is carved into the western side of its bare limestone slopes, and this can be seen from the road.

Crag Martin

Crag martins are often seen around mountain crags and in deep gorges. These aerobatic brown birds can be told from other martins and swallows by the wedge-shaped tail with its row of small, white blobs. Their close relative, the sand martin, has white underparts with a brown breast band.

Visitors should also look for jackdaws and ravens, the latter being easily told by their large size, jet-black plumage, wedge-shaped tail in flight and loud 'cronking' call. Ravens are impressive in flight but also worth watching because they mob birds of prey. Peregrines are the most usual species to be seen, but during spring and autumn migration periods, it is worth checking each raptor you see carefully because many other species pass through on passage.

The Líndos Peninsula

Set on the east side of Rhodes, this is the driest, hottest part of the island. Near the town of Líndos are dramatic sea cliffs and the famous acropolis. Here the cliffs drop sheer away to the azure waters of the Mediterranean. Before long, visitors will see crag martins feeding in small parties on the wing, hunting for insects close to the cliff face. They are sometimes seen in the company of swifts and the occasional alpine swift – the latter species has a white rump and throat and is considerably larger than its more common relative. In spring, blue rock thrushes sing their attractive song from rocky promontories along the cliff edge. Views stretch inland across large areas of *phrygana* habitat, characterised by low-growing plants and stony ground.

Cape Prasonísi

Cape Prasonísi lies at the southern tip of Rhodes and is a largely uninhabited and unspoilt region. The cape is connected to the mainland of Rhodes by a tombolo – a sand bar, covered only by the highest of tides – and the whole area is covered in excellent *phrygana* vegetation.

Jersey tiger moths in the Valley of the Butterflies, Petaloúdes

As you approach the cape from the main road, you drive across a flat, agricultural plain. The fields here are excellent for arable 'weeds' in the spring, and are very likely to contain both migrant and resident birds. Larks, pipits and wheatears feed on the ground, while bee-eaters perch on wires and birds of prey quarter the ground in search of insects and lizards. Having reached the sand tombolo, it is best to park before you reach the beach itself because the sand is extremely soft in places. The seas to the west of the beach are beloved of windsurfers. During periods of strong, onshore winds, seabirds also make use of the sea breezes, sometimes coming surprisingly close to shore. The *phrygana* vegetation which covers much of the cape is perhaps the best example of this habitat on the island. In spring, the dwarfed and flattened plants become studded with colourful flowers; cistuses, rosemary, thyme and spiny vetches are common.

The Valley of the Butterflies

The Valley of the Butterflies at Petaloúdes is world famous and attracts large numbers of tourists each year. Although the name is rather misleading – the 'butterflies' are in fact Jersey tiger moths – the name has stuck and thousands of people visit the site each year to witness the mass concentration of these insects during the hot summer months.

From the roadside car park, visitors pay to enter the site and then follow the streamside walk up the valley. The route is lined with oriental plane trees in which you may see birds such as robins, spotted flycatchers and wrens. There are fish in the deep pools and freshwater crabs scurry along the water's edge. Further up the valley, the crabs catch the moths, and their discarded wings can be seen beside the stream.

Because of the shade and humidity provided by the stream and the woodland, maidenhair fern flourishes beside the water. It is precisely these same environmental conditions, together with the supply of resin from the plane trees, that attract the Jersey tiger moths. Damp rock faces, tree trunks and branches and streamside boulders are covered with these attractive insects, which spend the dry summer months in the valley, departing only when the autumn rains arrive.

Sadly, tourism is having a detrimental effect on the moths: despite notices requesting visitors not to interfere with them, they are constantly disturbed and as a consequence fewer and fewer are seen each year. Hopefully, stricter enforcement of the notice may halt their decline. If you continue up the valley past the main concentrations of moths, the woodland gradually becomes less disturbed. Having crossed a road, the stream eventually dries up and as soon as the water disappears, so do the moths. The path eventually leads out of the valley and on to an old monastery. From here, good views can be had down the valley and visitors should look out for peregrines and ravens overhead.

The Valley of the Butterflies lies west of Maritsá, off the road from Kalamónas to Psínthos.

Kameíros Skála Castle

The Kastellos at Kameíros Skála (see page 64) is situated on the northwest coast near Kritiniá and is marked as an ancient monument on most maps of the island. In addition to its historic interest, the castle is surrounded by excellent woodland and maquis and there are inspiring views along the coast. Visitors should be aware, however, of military restrictions which apply to parts of the surrounding land and should take due note of the 'No Photography' signs.

The castle is reached along a stony path from the main coast road. The cliffs below the site are very steep and are the haunt of birds such as blue rock thrushes, crag martins, ravens and the occasional peregrine. However, it is the woodland and maquis which border the castle that are perhaps of more interest to the visiting naturalist. In spring, the flowers are colourful and varied. Tree heathers, brooms, juniper and cistuses are most conspicuous, but there are several species of orchids which can also be found by careful searching; giant orchid, sombre bee orchid and late spider orchid are among the most widespread. There are interesting plants to be found later in the season, one of the highlights being the beautiful flowers of caper, which can be found growing in the woods close to the ruins.

The Bay of Afántou

The sweeping Bay of Afántou (Órmos Afántou) lies south of Rhodes Town on the northeast coast between Cape (Akra) Ladikó and Cape Vágia. Although the southern parts of the bay are beginning to be developed for tourism, most of the shoreline is unspoilt and traditional farming and cultivation continues inland. The beach has maritime flowers, sea birds can be seen offshore, and inland, migrant and resident birds can be seen in olive groves and fields which are full of colourful flowers in spring. The beach which fringes the Bay of Afántou is surprisingly varied, with areas of sand, but also with shingle and boulders, which discourage many people. Spurges, yellow horned poppies and rock samphire can be found growing above the tideline and Kentish plovers grace the shoreline. These delightful little waders – grey on top and bright white below – are particularly attracted to areas of the bay where streams, which are dry for most of the year, come down to the beach.

The Southwest Coast

The southwest coast of Rhodes is fringed by an immense sandy beach. Because it is a long way from the centres of tourism and the prevailing onshore winds make the seas rough for much of the time, it is largely unexplored and undeveloped. Here, visitors

Purple spurge on a shingle beach

Bee-eaters
Inland fields bordered with sandy banks will attract bee-eaters. These colourful and aerobatic birds excavate burrows in the banks in which to nest, and their excited, bubbling calls are a familiar sound around the fields.
Their bright colours – vivid green, red ochre, yellow and black – make them exciting birds to spot. Bee-eaters specialise in catching insects on the wing and their graceful flight looks seemingly effortless as they glide and circle overhead.

can explore the beaches in isolation and find a wide range of wildlife, not only along the shoreline but also in the juniper scrub and maquis which lies inland.
A rough road (linking Apolakkiá with Kattavía) runs parallel with the beach for most of its length, but there are few stopping places and access to the shore is by the occasional gravel track.

Bird Migration
Many of the birds commonly found breeding in northern Europe during the summer months are not resident throughout the year but fly south each autumn to escape the winter and find better feeding. Some spend the winter around the Mediterranean but many fly further south to Africa. To avoid flying directly over the Mediterranean, millions of birds travel around the sea's eastern coast in spring and trickle along its northern shoreline, taking the reverse route each autumn. With Rhodes lying only a short distance from the Turkish coast, it is not surprising that large numbers pass through on spring and autumn migration and a good range of species can be found during these periods.
These include both summer breeding visitors to Rhodes and species *en route* to more northerly latitudes.
Spring migration begins in March and continues until May. Among the first birds to arrive are the martins – both house martins and sand martins will be seen – and swallows. Among the parties of swallows there are also likely to be the less widespread red-rumped swallows, which frequently associate with them. The latter species can be easily distinguished by its pale buffish-red rump and collar. Even on migration, birds tend to rest and feed in the habitats to which they are most suited. Thus, wheatears, larks and pipits can be found in arable fields and on bare ground, while warblers and flycatchers prefer scrub vegetation with plenty of cover. Among the larger birds, a wide range of birds of prey also migrate through the region – harriers, honey buzzards, lesser kestrels and the occasional red-footed falcon. They appear in both spring and autumn, which is also the case with rollers and bee-eaters. These two are without doubt the most colourful species to be seen on Rhodes and, fortunately, their habit of perching on wires and dead branches makes them easy to see.

FOOD AND DRINK

Sizzling meat in a psistaria

Because of the popularity of Rhodes among the Scandinavians and British, authentic, traditional Greek cuisine is almost impossible to find in the island's major holiday resorts. Instead, most tourist hotels and restaurants serve 'international' fare to please foreign tastes. Chicken, lamb chops, sausage-egg-and-chips and the like feature large, and there are often special children's menus. However, many establishments also offer Greek cuisine as an alternative, and this is often of a high standard. Restaurants and tavernas abound throughout the island, most of them representing reasonable value, although standards of service vary wildly. A smart appearance is by no means a good indication of quality – in fact, the more basic tavernas are often the best, especially if they are frequented by the locals. Even if you cannot understand the menu, you can always go into the kitchen and make a choice from the dishes you see being prepared. A *psistaria* specialises in meats grilled over charcoal, and, in resorts, may double as a fast food outlet serving pizzas, toasted sandwiches and hamburgers. In Rhodes Town you will also find small shops selling Greek fast food. Seafood (*psari*) such as lobster, crayfish, shrimps, squid and swordfish is the most expensive item on any menu, and for this reason is no longer the staple food of the locals: pollution and over-fishing have made prices rise. Although menus are often limited in choice, there is usually lamb, pork and chicken on offer.

Service with a smile in a taverna

Those unaccustomed to Greek food may find it a little greasy, and the islanders – like other Greeks – prefer their meals served warm rather than hot. Eating establishments are price controlled according to category, and though the service charge is included in the bill, it is customary to leave a little extra for the waiter.

Greek Cuisine
Menus are often in Greek, English, French, German and Swedish (with some bizarre translations). They will offer a limited choice that includes *mezedes* (hors d'oeuvres) and *tis oras* (meat and fish fried or grilled to order). What is on the menu will not necessarily be available – it is only a rough guide. The waiter will tell you what is 'on'.
Since the idea of courses is foreign to Greek cuisine, starters, main dishes and salads often arrive together.

The best thing is to order a selection of *mezedes* and salads to share among your party. The most interesting *mezedes* are *tzatziki* (yoghurt, garlic and cucumber dip); *melitzanosalata* (aubergine dip); courgettes or aubergines fried in batter; white haricot beans in vinaigrette sauce; *tiropitakia* or *spanakopites* (small cheese and spinach pies); *saganaki* (fried cheese); *oktapóthi* (octopus); *mavromatika* (black-eyed peas); and *dolmadakia* (vine leaves stuffed with meat or rice). Other typical *mezedes* are *garides* (shrimps), *feta* (white goat's cheese), *taramosalata* (pâte of smoked fish roe) and *bourekakia* (small meat pies). Greek salad (*horiatiki* to the Greeks) is a popular lunch choice. It consists of tomato and cucumber wedges, onion rings and red and green peppers, topped with *feta* and olives and sprinkled with oregano. Olive oil is usually added, but you could ask for it to be omitted. A simple tomato and cucumber salad is *angour domata*.

Meat Dishes

Shish kebab (*souvlákia*) and chops (*brizoles*) are usually reliable choices. The best *souvláki* is made from lamb (*arnisio*), but it is not often available. Nowadays these skewers of grilled meat, tomato, peppers and onions are often made with pork. The small lamb cutlets called *paidhákia* are usually very tasty, as is roast lamb (*arni psito*) and roast kid (*katsiki*), when obtainable. *Kefthedes* (meatballs), *biftekia* (a type of hamburger), and the spicy sausages called *loukanika* are usually good and cheap, although minced meat is the most common source of stomach problems in Rhodes as elsewhere, so it is important that such items are freshly made and thoroughly cooked. Restaurants with a fast turnover, and frequented by locals, are likely to be safe.

Another meat-based main course dish the visitor to Rhodes is likely to encounter is *moussaka*, a pie authentically made from aubergines and minced meat (preferably lamb, now often beef) topped with a custardy cheese sauce and baked. Among the many other tasty main courses found in tavernas are *pastitsio* (macaroni with minced meat and béchamel sauce), *gemista* (either tomatoes or green peppers stuffed with meat or rice), *yiouvarelákia* (stewed meatballs with rice), *souzoukákia* (meatballs with tomato sauce and garlic), *stifado* (meat with onions), *kokoretsi* (skewers of liver and kidneys) and *pastitsada* (tomato stew). *Youvetsi* is a veal casserole.

Fish

Coastal tavernas in Rhodes and many establishments in Rhodes Town, especially the medieval quarter, also offer fish and shellfish. *Kalamarákia* (fried baby squid) are widely available in summer, but the choice fish, such as red mullet (*barbounia*) and sea bream (*fangri*) are much less common and much more expensive. Among the fish and seafood dishes fairly widely available are *astakós* (lobster), *midia* (mussels), *lithrinia* (bass), *glossa* (sole) and *marídes* (whitebait). Less pricey but equally tasty are *xifhias*, grilled pieces of swordfish served on skewers with onions, tomatoes and bay leaves. The price of fish is quoted by the kilo, and the standard procedure is to 'go to the glass' (which may mean a tank or refrigerator) and choose your own.

Desserts

Restaurants catering for tourists may serve a limited choice of desserts, but after a meal most Greeks prefer to go to a *zaharoplastion* (pâtisserie), where sticky, sweet confections are served with a glass of water, or may be taken out in a box. Fruit is often the most delicious dessert. Watermelon (*karpouzi*) and *peponi* (a melon with a somewhat unusual taste) are the standard summer fruit, along with peaches, oranges, figs and seedless grapes. You will also find ice cream (*pagotó*), often home-made and usually creamy and very good. Yoghurt with honey is a simple and delicious finish to a meal. Other desserts include *pastes* (very sweet cakes with cream), *baklavá* (syrup cake with nuts), *loukoumádes* (fritters with honey or syrup), and *kataifi* (shredded wheat soaked in honey). One of Rhodes' specialities is *rizogalo*, cold rice pudding flavoured with lemon and cinnamon. You can usually find it in Rhodes Town at a *galaktopolio*, a dairy counter selling items such as yoghurt, milk, butter and pastries.

Snacks

Traditional snacks are one of the delights of Greek cuisine, although they are being increasingly replaced by international favourites such as toasted sandwiches (*tost*), and pizzas. However, small kebabs (*souvlákia*) can sometimes be found in Rhodes, especially in Rhodes Town, and cheese pies (*tiropites*) can almost always be found at the baker's. Another popular snack is *yiro* (doner kebab) served in pitta bread with garnish.

Drinks

Wine (*krasi*) is commonly drunk on Rhodes. White is *aspro krasi*, red is *mavro krasi*, and both leave that unique Greek aftertaste which you either love or hate. Acceptable local wines include Líndos Blanc Sec and Grand Maître (both white) and Chevalier de Rhodes, a red wine.

Retsina, a wine flavoured with pine resin, which comes from mainland Greece, should be served chilled and is available from bottles or from barrels. Unresinated Demesticha is available as white or red, and is inexpensive.

Greek brandy (*koniak*) can be dreadful or excellent; cheaper brands tend to be rather sweet, while the well-known brands (usually more reliable) are Botrys, Metaxa and Cambas, of which different qualities are produced. Imported spirits and drinks such as whisky, gin and vermouth are usually more expensive than locally produced equivalents. Beer (*bira*) in Rhodes usually means lager, though Guinness and Newcastle Brown may be found in some bars. Amstel, Henninger and Heineken, all brewed in Greece under licence, are cheaper than imported brands and just as good. Soft drinks (*anapsiktika*) such as Coca-Cola and Seven Up are available everywhere, as are various brands of mineral water. The Greek soft drinks tend to be very sweet and syrupy; *Portokalada* is a fizzy orange drink, and the cloudy-looking *limonada* has a real taste of lemon. Many bars serve freshly squeezed orange juice, and you can buy pure orange juice at mini-markets. Instant coffee – referred to simply as *nes* (short for Nescafé) – is widely available if

Yiros and pitta bread is the favourite Rhodian fast food

the strong, thick Greek coffee is not to your liking, but specify when ordering. Unless you specify hot (*zestó*) coffee you will be served *frappé* (iced), with or without milk. Coffee is traditionally taken on its own by most Greeks, particularly after a meal, and is normally accompanied by a glass of water. Greek coffee comes very sweet (*glyko*) unless you ask for it be medium (*metrio*) or without sugar (*sketo*). You may find espresso in some of the more expensive cafés, while Scandinavian versions of coffee can be found in the new section of Rhodes Town. Tea is not widely drunk, but is available in tourist areas, though seldom accompanied by milk.

A popular pre-dinner drink is *ouzo*, the national aperitif – a clear, aniseed-flavoured spirit similar to Turkish *raki*. It is most commonly served mixed with cold water, when it turns a milky colour, but you can also have it neat or with ice.

SHOPPING

The Dodecanese islands no longer enjoy the special duty-free status which they were granted on their union with Greece in 1947. However, shopping on Rhodes is still excellent value.

Some of the most popular souvenirs include leather bags and purses, brass and copper ware, worry beads (*komboloi*) of all sizes and materials, costume dolls, woven bedspreads, rugs and bags, shirts and dresses. Prices are fixed in major shops and fashionable boutiques, but a little haggling – especially if you are buying several items in one shop – is considered the norm in the smaller shops.

Rhodians are proud of their plates

Clothes
Major brand denim wear is cheaper than elsewhere in Europe, as are fashion names like Sishey and Benetton. Shops specialising in sportswear include **Sportivo**, 22 Odos G Griva, and **Rhodos Sport**, 15 Ethelondon Dodecanision; and in tee-shirts **Illusion T Shirts**, Odos 25 Martíou.

Flowers
An excellent reasonably priced flower shop, operated by the Municipality of Rhodes, can be found at Mandraki Harbour. It is open daily 07.00 to 14.30hrs.

Handicrafts
Embroidered tablecloths and clothes, and articles carved out of olivewood or onyx make popular souvenirs and are available throughout the island.

Jewellery
Goldsmiths and silversmiths have been practising their craft on Rhodes for 4,000 years, and there is an excellent choice available today, ranging from copies of jewellery made by ancient craftsmen to modern designs. The elaborate silver filigree jewellery of Rhodes, set with semi-precious stones imported from Italy, and made into rings, brooches, necklaces and other jewellery, is particularly distinctive and attractive. There are numerous jewellery shops throughout the island, especially in Rhodes Town. **M Mentos**, at 34 Odos Apellou, in the Old Town, and **J Frantzis**, with branches at 103 Odos Sokrátous and 19 Odos Aristotelous, also in the Old Town, have good selections.

Lace
Handmade lace is beautiful but expensive, especially that from Líndos, but beware of factory-made imitations.

Leather
Handmade leather peasant boots from the village of Archángelos can be bought either there, or in Rhodes Town. They are very popular, not least because they are so comfortable. A good selection of leather handbags, belts and wallets can be found at **Telhines**, which has two shops in Rhodes Town – at 36/38 Odos G Griva, and 10 Odos Orfeos.

Pottery
Pottery from Líndos is particularly attractive, especially the brightly coloured, decorative plates. But there are ceramic factories throughout the island which supply items to shops in all the main resorts, so there is a good choice everywhere. Most popular souvenirs, apart from plates, are vases and ashtrays. Blue tends to be the predominant colour, and designs are often based on deer, ships or flowers.

Photographic Equipment
Brouzakis, 47 Odos Sof Venizelou, Rhodes Town, has a good selection of photographic equipment, including lenses, adaptors and various types of filters. A quick film development service is also available.

Shoes
Fashionable shoes are made on the island. Those made for export are of a higher quality and make an excellent buy. Also good are leather slippers which have a reputation for being extremely hard wearing and long lasting. **Moshoutis**, in Odos D Theoraki, has a good choice, as do the various branches of the chain **'24'**, found in Ammokhoustou, Karpathou and Makariou streets.

Spirits
All the better-known international brands of whisky, brandy, gin and other spirits and liqueurs can be bought relatively cheaply. **Cava Arapoudis**, 13 Odos Gallias, Rhodes Town, is one of many outlets offering a good selection.

Lace-seller, Líndos

Umbrellas
Colourful imported umbrellas and parasols are for sale practically everywhere. There is a good selection on offer at the **Umbrella Factory**, 41 Odos Karpathou, Rhodes Town.

Wood
Olive-wood salad bowls, carving boards, mortars and pestles are worth seeking out in the better gift/souvenir shops.

Those who enjoy the hustle and bustle of markets should note that there are two in Rhodes Town – the Old Market (Palia Agorá), within the medieval walled city; and the larger New Market (Neá Agorá) at Mandraki Harbour.

ACCOMMODATION

Hotels

Hotels in Rhodes are classified according to the size of their rooms and public areas, the décor and furnishings of the rooms, and the facilities and service provided. 'Deluxe', 'A' and 'B' grade hotels have dining facilities on the premises; grade 'C' do not. Moves are currently under way by the Greek government to introduce a star system for hotels on the mainland and the islands in a bid to raise standards. Fears have also been expressed by many travel industry experts of the threat of too many hotels on Rhodes and other major Greek holiday islands. However, plans for hundreds of new establishments in Rhodes and neighbouring islands have been put on hold in recent years because of a sharp drop in the number of visitors from Britain and Germany.
Hotel reservations can be made through a travel agent or airline, by writing to the hotel direct, or by contacting the Hotel Owners' Association of Rhodes, 3 Odos Platia Plessa, Rhodes Town (tel: 26446).
If you arrive in Rhodes without accommodation, your best bet is to ask at the tourist office.

Pensions

A-Class *pensions* are listed by the National Tourist Organisation. Many are recently built, with en-suite facilities in bright, comfortable rooms, and represent excellent value for money. They are to be found throughout the island, but are mainly in the north.

Líndos, looking towards the sea

Rooms

A popular choice with independent travellers is to rent a room in a private house. The best of these are now listed by the NTOG. Rooms are generally clean, though with basic bathroom facilities. The option of a breakfast is sometimes made for a small additional charge. Beds may not be of the type most visitors are accustomed to. This is especially true in the resort of Líndos where, in common with local traditions and habits, they are usually of the wooden platform type on which one or two mattresses are placed. A good night's sleep is not guaranteed!
The government-approved and categorised rooms are slightly more expensive than rooms in

other households, but are of a reliable standard. This type of accommodation is seasonal, available mostly from May to September.

Self-catering

Eating out on Rhodes is cheap and good value so the freedom of a self-catering holiday can be fully appreciated. The NTOG's guide to tour operators lists companies offering self-catering accommodation.

The standards of accommodation on the island in self-catering properties are not comparable with those in other Mediterranean countries. Most tour operators try to ensure acceptable standards are maintained and that the accommodation offered is clean and comfortable, but luxuries such as electric kettles, toasters, irons and a vast choice of kitchen utensils will almost certainly not be included in the equipment provided in self-catering apartments and studios. Many apartments rely on solar heating systems; some have an electrical back-up system which is used only in bad weather. It is often necessary to contact the caretaker or owner if the weather is such that the electrical system needs to be used.

It has become standard practice for proprietors to ask to keep your passport, ostensibly for the police but in reality to prevent you leaving with an unpaid bill. Some owners may be satisfied with just taking down the details and they will almost always return the documents if you need them.

Water is a valuable commodity in Rhodes, especially in the height of the summer, and visitors should expect an occasional drop in water pressure. An increasing number of proprietors rely on solar power to heat the water. In such cases, when the sun is not shining, shortages of hot water have to be accepted.

Camping

Rhodes, with its wonderful climate, is ideal for camping. There are two campsites on the island. **Faliraki Camping** (tel: 85358), is peacefully located just outside the lively resort of Faliráki some 16km (10 miles) from Rhodes Town. It enjoys a splendid position amid terraced hills and affords good open views towards the inland range of hills, especially from the well-sited swimming pool and sun terraces.

Beside the pool is a disco-bar

and restaurant with covered drinking terrace. There is also a supermarket for daily provisions and a lounge area with TV and video. On-site facilities also include clean shower and toilet blocks, a laundry, and a kitchen complete with stoves and seating area.
Near by, evening entertainment can be found in the bustling bars, nightclubs and restaurants of Faliráki, and the excellent beaches at Ladikó, Afàntou and Faliráki are within easy reach for daytime relaxation. There is a bus service to Rhodes Town and to local facilities.
A second campsite, **Aghios Georghios** (Tel: 44203) is on the beach just outside Lárdos.

ENTERTAINMENT AND NIGHTLIFE

Most principle resorts on Rhodes have discothèques aimed mainly at younger visitors; this is especially so in Rhodes Town, Líndos, Faliráki and Ixós.
The majority of resorts also have a range of bars, from simple to stylish, with cocktail bars especially numerous.
Folklore shows are staged frequently throughout the island, and versions of *Zorba the Greek* or Sirtaki dances can be seen in numerous tavernas, where the waiters will be happy to teach you a few basic steps. But you will soon want to sit down and admire when the professional dancers take to the floor and give more elaborate performances, often including dancing in a ring of fire and lifting tables with their teeth.

Plate Smashing

As a sign of appreciation, happiness and high spirits, the Greeks may start to smash their plates on the floor. Officially, plate smashing has been declared illegal as it was considered likely to encourage rioting, but it can be seen at nightclubs and restaurants with special licences that allow the smashing of unglazed pottery. Plate smashing can be a wonderful way of letting off steam – but do not get carried away, since you are charged for each and every plate you break!

Cinemas

There are six cinemas in Rhodes Town, including (summer only) the **Rodon**, to the rear of the National Theatre; the **Dimotikon**, in Odos 25 Martíou; the **Metropol**, on Vyronós, Vass Friderikis, Dimokratías and the junction with Stefanou Casouli; and in the winter months the **Titania-Palace** on Odos Kolokotroni east of the stadium. They show a mix of Greek and foreign films, accompanied by Greek subtitles.
Summer performances: 18.00–20.00, 20.00–22.00, and 22.00–24.00hrs; winter performances: 17.30–19.30, 19.30–21.30 and 21.30–23.30hrs. On Sundays and holidays performances usually start at 15.00hrs.

Discos

There are numerous discos centred on and around Plateía Akadimías, in Rhodes Town, as well as Iroon Polytechniou, which branches north of Plateía

Akadimías and nearby Odos Alexandrou Diakou. The other major resorts on the island also have discothèques.

Casino

If you like a flutter, there is one casino on Rhodes – at the Grand Hotel Astir Palace, in Rhodes Town. Here you can try your luck at American roulette, blackjack, *chemin-de-fer* and baccarat. There are also numerous slot machines. A passport is necessary to gain admittance, and dress must be smart – men must wear a shirt with collar.

Folk Shows

The **Greek Dance Group**, founded by Nelly Dimoglou, gives daily performances (except on Saturdays) of folk dances and songs in the **Old Theatre,** Odos Andronicou, Rhodes Town, from May to October. Times of performances should be checked with the NTOG office or the Municipal Tourist Office. The **National Theatre**, located at Mandraki Harbour, in the New Town, hosts plays and ballets based on folk customs, such as a wedding or the departure of sponge fishermen. Visiting companies from the National Theatre in Athens and the Athenian Festival also give performances here during the summer months.

Dancing the night away

WEATHER AND WHEN TO GO

The climate of Rhodes is excellent most of the year, although the island is generally regarded as a summer holiday destination only, with the result that most hotels, restaurants, tavernas and bars close during the winter months.
Nevertheless, severe weather is a rarity, even in the coldest months – January and February (averaging 54°F/12°C). The most popular time for a holiday here is between July and August, but you can usually be sure of near-constant sunshine any time from May to October. In high summer, however, the climate is never unbearably hot, thanks to the *meltemi*, a northwest wind which provides a cool breeze, particularly on the west coast. An out-of-season visit – in April/May when the spring flowers are still blooming or September/October after the rush of visitors has left – has a great deal to recommend it.

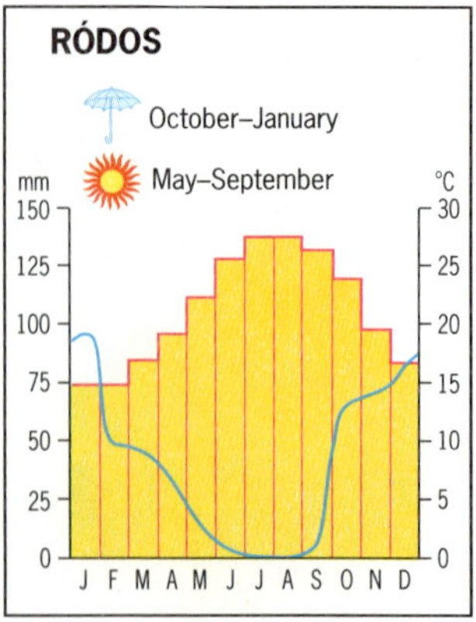

What to Take and Wear

Good sunglasses are vital, as is suntan cream providing a good barrier to harmful ultra-violet rays. Clothing should be light, comfortable and casual, although more formal wear may be required at some of the more up-market hotels, especially in the evenings, and also if you plan to visit the casino in Rhodes Town. Bathing shoes are useful to avoid cuts from some of the rocky, pebbly beaches, and comfortable footwear advisable for those who intend to visit any of the ancient sites or undertake long walks. Sweaters are also advisable for most of the year, since the nights can be cool.

HOW TO BE A LOCAL

Rhodians have a short fuse. They rarely lose their tempers with visitors, but with fellow Greeks it is a different matter. You are likely to hear more than a few shouting matches, though tempers invariably cool as quickly as they flared. They are also hard workers and early risers – a fact that is lost on most late-rising visitors, who see islanders lingering through the hot afternoon at their favourite café, chatting and watching the world go by. In fact, many of them are enjoying a long midday break after starting work at sunrise, and will go back to work for several hours in the evening.
A good place to join the locals is at the New Market in Rhodes Town, or at one of the pastry/coffee shops in Rhodes Town, or any of the

unpretentious pavement cafés in the less-developed resorts. Rhodians love food but eat out only on special occasions avoiding the 'touristy' restaurants in favour of simpler, less-sophisticated tavernas. These are usually found in side streets or alleys – and this is where to search if you are looking for genuine local cuisine that is reasonably priced. When Greeks go out to dine they do so late. To enjoy their company, don't start dinner until at least 22.00hrs. They also love fish, which they buy from the fish stalls in the Neá Agorá (New Market) in Rhodes Town, directly from the quayside at several of the island's fishing villages, such as Kameíros Skála, or from vans which visit most of the bigger villages every weekday morning. Visitors who share their enjoyment of fish, and are staying in self-catering accommodation, would be well advised to follow suit.

Think First
Nudism is against Greek law, even though topless sunbathing is tolerated in most 'tourist' resorts on the island. However, should you decide to strip, your action could result in a fine or even lead to a prison sentence. The Rhodians are a modest people, and visitors should have regard for local custom.

For getting out and about, the locals on the island of Rhodes rely heavily on buses which, though somewhat erratic, are frequent and cheap, so if you want to do some exploring, it makes sense to follow their example. Buses also let you see the traditional side of Rhodes, as they potter through remote villages.

Locals travel at their own pace. Donkeys and mules are still in everyday use

Scooters and motorcycles are also popular means of transport and are readily available for rent. Although helmets should be worn by law, few do so and they are seldom provided, so if you value your life this is the one case where it is not wise to follow local habits.

It is considered bad form for men or women to wear shorts in churches or museums. Women should also wear a headscarf in church.

CHILDREN

Restaurants and cafés do their best to accommodate children

Rhodes is popular with people with children and is well equipped to cater for them. Many hotels have separate children's swimming pools, or areas of the main pool reserved for their use, and some of the larger establishments have children's play areas and offer special menus and programmes of games and activities. High chairs and early dinners are also widely available. A large number of hotels on the islands have three-sided lifts (ie with no inner door), a danger to unsupervised children. These have been mentioned in hotel descriptions throughout the book. Many of the island's beaches offer safe bathing, and are well equipped with water-sports facilities. Parents should take note, however, that the cooling west-coast wind can mask high temperatures, so that they may underrate the power of the sun. Children should be protected from sunburn at all times and should wear a hat.

At night, children are fascinated with the special Greek evenings and particularly enjoy the opportunity for some intentional plate smashing! (See page 100.)

Burgers and fries feature on many menus. Pizza and spaghetti are also widely available. The Greeks love children, so there is no problem in taking them out with you.

It should not be necessary to bring baby requisites with you, as the shops on Rhodes can supply the usual items, such as disposable napkins.

Many hotels provide baby listening or babysitting services. Such facilities have been mentioned in the descriptions of individual hotels in the book. Check that the service is available before booking.

TIGHT BUDGET

As is the case with many holiday destinations, Rhodes is cheapest in the low seasons. Most of the hotels, restaurants and bars on the island are closed during the winter months – though, surprisingly, the museums and the ancient sites remain open – so the best time to enjoy a holiday on Rhodes, and save on expense, is in the spring and autumn, when rates are considerably less than during the peak months of July and August.

Where to Stay

You can also cut the cost of a holiday in Rhodes by opting for self-catering accommodation. The island offers a wide range of apartments and studios for holiday rental, especially in the smaller, less-developed resorts, and most of them are available through overseas tour operators. These are invariably cheaper than hotels, especially if several adults are sharing.

An inexpensive option for the lone traveller, or couple, is to stay in a *pension* or rent a room in a private house. Another tip is to avoid the well-developed resorts and choose instead one of the lesser-known, off-the-beaten-track places. Not only will you find these offer less expensive accommodation, but prices in restaurants and bars are usually lower than in the more popular, livelier resorts.

Where to Eat

To save on restaurant bills, seek out the less-expensive self-service restaurants and cafeterias. The market in Rhodes Town has cheap tavernas. In general, the best-value taverna is where you see locals eating. A picnic lunch of bread, cheese and fruit is cheap – and healthy. Or you can go for some of the delicious take-away snacks, available from bakers – for example, *tiropites* (cheese pies) are excellent.

Getting About

Buses are a cheap mode of transport and cover the whole island. However, in season they tend to be very crowded, and out of season services are much less regular.

Taxis are not such an expensive alternative as in many other places – especially when shared. Fix a price with the driver before setting off.

Scooter or moped rental is not too costly and a practical way of getting to see everything. See **Directory – Driving** for more information.

In Brief

- Travel out of high season.
- Avoid popular resorts.
- Stay in *pensions*, private rooms or self-catering accommodation.
- Eat where the locals go.
- Use public transport.

SPECIAL EVENTS

1 January. On New Year's Day – or St Basil's Day as it is also known – visitors might be offered sprigs of the herb basil, named after the saint, as a symbol of hospitality.

6 January. Epiphany Day, marked by the blessing of water throughout Greece. In Rhodes Town a cross blessed by a bishop is dropped into the harbour and young swimmers try to retrieve it, while white pigeons are released to fly over the area. The person to surface with the cross is anointed with oil, blessed, and given coins.

February. Carnival time, with floats, fancy dress and merry-making in Rhodes Town, Archángelos, Apóllona and the village of Kameíros Skála.

Easter. This is the most important festival of the Greek Orthodox Church. For the three weeks preceding Lent, there are colourful processions and raucous parties, with the revellers donning costumes and masks. The first Monday of Lent, known as Clean Monday, is a day of fasting when some people eat only garlic mashed with potatoes. On Good Friday a solemn, silent procession takes place in Rhodes Town, while Holy Saturday marks the beginning of Easter. Church bells peal, fireworks are set off, and worshippers exchange Easter greetings.

25 March. Greek Independence Day. This is a national holiday with parades and folk dancing.

1 May. May Day, when garlands of flowers are hung on door-knobs, often by lovers. They usually remain in place for many weeks.

15 May. A giant street market, fiesta and funfair is held on this day to mark the Festival of the Virgin Mary.

24 June. The feast of St John the Baptist, celebrated everywhere with bonfires.

June. The last 10 days mark the island's annual summer celebrations, with beauty contests, folk dancing and singing.

July. The first week is Naval Week, with open-air concerts and fireworks as well as boat races.

30 July. In honour of St Saul (Silas), a big celebration is held near the village of Soroní. Saul is said to have been a companion of St Paul and to have performed miracles. The celebrations are lively, and include donkey racing and folk dancing.

6 August and throughout the month. Dance festivals take place in the villages of Maritsá, Kalithiés and Embonas.

15 August. Assumption Day, the most renowned festival in the Dodecanese, with week-long dancing and religious processions in Kremastí and Triánta.

8 September. Birth of the Virgin Mary. At Tsampíka, on the eve of this holy day, childless women make a pilgrimage up the steep hill to the monastery to pray for fertility.

28 October. Parades, folk dances and other celebrations are held throughout the island to mark the Greek victory over Fascist Italy in 1940.

SPORT

Rhodes offers a good choice of sporting and recreational activities, ranging from excellent watersports to hiking and golf.

Boating

If you are a competent sailor and wish to take a boat out for a day or longer, you can apply to the Nautical Club of Rhodes (NCR), at 9 Plateía Kountouriótou (near the Elli Beach Club), tel: 23287. It is important to remember, however, that the unpredictable north wind known as the *meltemi* can make sailing in small boats quite tricky.

Fishing

Spear-fishing is very popular on the island, and you do not need a permit. However, you are not allowed to practise the sport within 100 yards (90m) of a public beach, and any fish you spear must weigh more than 150 grams. You can snorkel freely anywhere along the coast, but for sub-aqua sports you need to join the diving school in Rhodes harbour. The best fishing grounds tend to be off the shores of Líndos, Kameíros, Kallithéa and Gennádio, and fishing tackle can be bought in the Neá Agorá, Rhodes Town.

Sitting on the dock of a bay

Golf

There is only one golf course on Rhodes, an 18-hole course situated at Afántou village, just over 12 miles (20km) from Rhodes Town (tel: 51255). Facilities include a clubhouse, changing rooms, and a snack bar. Clubs can be hired, and green fees are not expensive by international standards. Many hotels on the east and west coasts have mini-golf courses, which can also be found in Rhodes Town (near the Palm Hotel) and on the west coast (near the Metropolitan Capsis Hotel) where visitors not staying in hotels can play.

Horse Riding

Mikes Stables, inland from Kalithiés village, about nine miles (15km) from Rhodes Town.

Hunting

A licence is required to hunt game or animals, such as wild duck, hares and partridges. Applications should be made to the **Hunting Club of Rhodes**, Municipal Marketplace, 1st Floor, No 7 (tel: 21841). The hunting season runs from 25 August to 10 March for migratory birds, and from 1 November to 10 January for rabbits and partridges. Although the deer population is quite large, they are protected by law, and cannot be hunted.

Tennis

Numerous hotels on the island have their own tennis courts. Visitors staying in smaller, less well-equipped hotels, can play at the **Rhodes Town Tennis Club** (tel: 25705) located at 20 Vassileos Konstantinou, facing Elli Beach. This welcomes all non-nationals who wish to play. There are seven courts in total, of which two are clay and the remainder cement. The courts are open between 09.00 and 20.00hrs. Players must wear tennis clothes – swimsuits are not allowed. Racquets and balls are available for hire.

Walking

In the spring and autumn Rhodes is an ideal island for walking, providing routes for both serious ramblers and those who like a gentle stroll. There is a dearth of official information but an invaluable source of information is Noel Rochford's *Landscapes of Rhodes* (Sunflower Books).

Water Sports

Most of the island's popular beaches offer facilities for windsurfing, waterskiing and para-skiing. There is an excellent windsurfing school – the **Surfers Paradise** – opposite the Hilton Hotel, Ixós, and others at Faliráki Beach and near the Líndhos Bay Hotel. Pedaloes can be hired at most beaches. The east coast is more suited to waterskiing than the west, the sea and wind here being calmer. Swimming is understandably the most popular of all water sports, and is best practised at resorts such as Faliráki, whose beach slopes gently out to sea, making it an ideal swimming spot for children; Líndos, where there are excellent changing facilities and showers; or Lárdos Bay, where the long, sandy beach is less crowded.

DIRECTORY

Contents

Arriving

By Air

Although a few scheduled airlines operate direct, non-stop flights from European cities to Rhodes, the majority of flights are routed via Athens, with onward connections to Rhodes. At Athens, Olympic Airways operates from the west air terminal of the Hellenikon airport. If you arrive on a foreign airline, take one of the frequent buses from the east air terminal. The flight from Athens to Rhodes takes about one and a half hours. In addition to the scheduled flights, numerous companies operate package holidays to Rhodes incorporating a direct charter flight and accommodation in either hotels or self-catering apartments, studios, or village rooms. All flights to Rhodes land at Rhodes International Airport, which is located at Paradhísion, about 10 miles (16km) from Rhodes Town. It has all the usual facilities of a busy airport, including a tourist office.
From the airport you can reach Rhodes Town either by bus or taxi. The latter are easy to obtain and are reasonably priced, but it is wise to confirm the price in advance.
Olympic Airways' buses have the edge over the public variety because they have greater luggage capacity. Public buses run every 45 minutes from 06.30 to 22.30hrs. Porters are available to carry bags to the taxi rank or bus stop. If you wish to use the Olympic Airways bus to take you to the airport on your journey home, you must wait in front of the airline's office at 19 Odos Ierou Lohou (tel: 24571) at least two hours before the flight departure time.

By Sea

There are sea routes to Athens from Genoa, Venice, Ancona, Naples, Brindisi, Bari and Marseilles. Vessels operating on these routes are generally large passenger ships, many equipped to carry cars. Rhodes and other islands of the Dodecanese are served by scheduled passenger and car-ferry boats from

Leather goods are popular souvenirs

Piraeus, the port of Athens. Frequency varies according to the season. In the peak months one or more vessels a day leave for Rhodes, taking around 14 hours. Some of these also carry cargo, so be prepared for delays when loading or unloading. The services tend to be extremely busy, and cabins should be booked well in advance, even in the low season.

By Road

Land–sea routes to Rhodes across Europe are not the quickest or most comfortable means of reaching the island and in recent years have been interrupted by the conflicts in the former Yugoslavia. It is possible to drive to Ancona in Italy, where you can take a ferry to Patras in Western Greece, then drive to Athens. This takes four to five days from the UK.

By Rail

You can travel to Rhodes by a combination of rail and ship, but it is not really recommended. The most direct route, through the former Yugoslavia, has not yet been fully restored following the conflict in Bosnia and Croatia.

Entry Formalities

A passport but no visa is required for visitors to Rhodes from West European countries (including UK citizens), Australia, New Zealand, Canada, the USA and the Irish Republic. Visitors from EU countries with ID cards do not need a passport.

Visas are also generally not required by: military persons travelling on a Military Identity Card (with movement or leave order) issued by NATO; holders of a re-entry permit provided that they hold official documents proving their residence in Greece; holders of tickets with onward reservations provided that their journey to a third country will commence within 48 hours from arrival. Check regulations before your journey. If you want to stay

longer than three months you should officially apply for an extension. However, visitors from EU countries need not do this. In Rhodes this can be done through the local police. It is advisable to complete this procedure a couple of weeks before your time runs out and also keep all your pink, personalised bank exchange slips as confirmation that you can subsist without working.
If you plan to visit Turkey from Rhodes there are one or two important rules to follow to avoid re-entry or exit problems. Check with a local travel agent or tour operator's representative.

Camping
The island has two campsites, which have good amenities including shops, sports and entertainment facilities. (See page 99 for details). Note that it is illegal to camp outside official campsites.

Chemists see **Pharmacies**

Crime
Crime is rare on Rhodes, but it is still wise to take precautions such as depositing valuables in the hotel safe, if available, and taking care of your possessions when in public, especially on the beach or when shopping. In the event of theft contact the police at Etgelondon Dodekanissiou, Rhodes Town (tel: 27423), or your nearest police station.
Drug offences can lead to heavy sentences. Other activities that can get the unwary traveller into trouble are nudity, taking photographs in sensitive areas such as military barracks (marked with a camera crossed through) and abusing the Greek flag.
See also **Driving – Regulations** for certain legal requirements to be observed by motorists.

Customs
Visitors aged 18 years and over are allowed to import free of duty the following items:
If arriving from EU countries: 800 cigarettes **or** 200 cigars **or** 400 cigarillos **or** 1,000 grams of tobacco; ten litres of alcohol **or** 20 litres of wine, sparkling wine or liqueurs; 75 grams of perfume and three-eighths of a litre of toilet water; 1,000 grams of coffee **or** 375 grams of coffee extract; 200 grams of tea **or** 80 grams of tea extract.
If arriving from non-EU countries: 200 cigarettes **or** 50 cigars **or** 100 cigarillos **or** 250 grams of tobacco; one litre of alcohol **or** two litres of wine, sparkling wine or liqueurs; 50 grams of perfume and a quarter of a litre of toilet water; 500 grams of coffee **or** 200 grams of coffee extract; 100 grams of tea **or** 40 grams of tea extract.
Visitors to Greece may, as a general rule, temporarily import personal articles duty-free, providing they are considered as being in use and in keeping with the personal status of the importer. Plants with soil are prohibited. Cats and dogs require health and rabies inoculation certificates issued by a veterinary authority in the country of origin not more than 12 months (cats six months) and not less than six days prior to arrival.

Importation of antiquities and works of art is free but they should be declared, together with their value, so that they may be freely exported. It is forbidden to export antiquities and works of art found in Greece. The duty-free allowance for goods exported from Greece will depend upon the traveller's nationality and the import regulations of the country of their destination, which should be determined before departure.

Disabled People
Virtually no specific provision is made, and hardly any accommodation is built with access needs in mind. The National Tourist Organisation of Greece should have details of specialist travel companies if local travel agencies are unable to help.

Driving
Main roads are usually asphalted, but it is folly to drive at speed. Curves are not usually signposted and seldom banked, so great care is required. Secondary roads are sometimes very rough, and are often narrow, serpentine and steep. Greece has the second worst road fatality rate in Europe (after Portugal).

Fuel
Filling stations are open from 07.00 to 19.00hrs Monday to Saturday, and they operate a rota system to cover evenings until midnight and Sundays. There is always a station open somewhere near Rhodes Town, but out of town supplies are patchy. Petrol (leaded) is sold as Venzini Apli (91–92 octane) and Venzini Super (96–98 octane). Unleaded petrol is sold as Super (95 and 98 octane) at stations displaying the sign. The acceptance of credit cards for petrol purchases is limited.

Regulations
Vehicles are driven on the right-hand side of the road and, unless otherwise indicated by signs, cars are subject to the following speed restrictions: 31mph (50kph) in built-up areas; 56mph (90kph) outside built-up areas; and 68mph (110kph) on dual-carriageways. Seat belts must be worn by law – though many rented cars are not even fitted with them. It is also compulsory to carry a warning triangle, fire extinguisher and a first-aid kit – failure to comply may result in a fine. Children are not allowed to travel in the front seat of a car, and it is an offence to carry a petrol can in a car.

Rental
Bicycles, mopeds, motorcycles and cars are popular means of exploring the island and are readily available in Rhodes Town, Faliráki, Triánta, Líndos and several smaller resorts. There is no shortage of rental firms, including well-known companies such as Avis and Hertz in Rhodes Town, and local firms in all the major resorts. No licence is required for mopeds or motorcycles up to 50cc, but helmets are rarely provided and riding is risky. It is important to remember that the basic insurance offered on the hire of mopeds or motorcycles provides only third-party

insurance cover – meaning that neither rider nor bike is covered – so drivers should take out a comprehensive policy, especially in view of the poor state of many of the roads. Most companies have clauses in their conditions of hire which stipulate that their insurance is invalidated if you travel on non-tarmac roads (many sites can be reached only on rough tracks). It should also be noted that motorcycles are not allowed in towns after 23.00hrs. For driving on Rhodes a valid pink EU licence, which includes translations, is acceptable. An International Driving Permit (IDP) is advisable for holders of other licences, such as the British green licence, because these do not carry translations. An IDP is also required for nationals of the US, Canada and Australia. The IDP must be obtained from a motoring club at home. A registration document and EU or UK insurance are sufficient for temporarily imported vehicles. To drive your own imported car or motorcycle over 50cc, the minimum age is 17, but you have

Would-be easy riders should use extreme caution on island roads

Bright lights and quiet streets

to be 23 years old to rent a vehicle, though many companies do not stick rigidly to this rule.

Electricity
The voltage in Rhodes, as in the rest of Greece, is 220 volts. Transformers are not usually required, but as plugs are of the common European two-pin type, an adaptor may be necessary in order to use a shaver or hairdryer. Street lights are scarce in many parts of the island, so it is useful to take a torch with you, especially if you are staying in an apartment or *pension* off the beaten track.

Embassies and Consulates
There are a number of West European consulates on Rhodes, but the USA, Australia, New Zealand, Canada and the Republic of Ireland do not have consulates here.

Australia: 37 Dimitriou Soutsou Street, Ambelokipi, Athens (tel: 644-7303)
Canada: 4 Ioannou, Gennadiou Street, Athens (tel: 725-4011)
New Zealand: 9 Semitelou Street, Athens 11528 (tel: 771-0112)
Republic of Ireland: 7 Leoforos Vasileos, Konstantinou, Athens (tel: 723-2771)
UK: 23 Odos 25 Martiou, Rhodes Town (tel: 27306/27247)
USA: Vas Sofia 91, Athens (tel: 721-2951).

Emergency Telephone Numbers
Police: 100
Fire: 199
Ambulance: 166
Hospital emergency: 25555
Greek Automobile Association: 351200

Entertainment Information

The English-language *Rhodes Gazette*, published from April to the end of October, contains information on local events and entertainment, and is available free from newsagents and tourist offices.

Health

There are no required inoculations for Rhodes, or other parts of Greece, but ensure you are up to date on tetanus and polio. British (upon production of Department of Health form E111) and other EU nationals are entitled to free medical care, but this means admittance only to the lowest grade of hospital, and does not include nursing care. In any case, treatment and prescribed medicines are first paid for and the costs are then refunded by the Greek authorities. If you require prolonged medical care or are from a country outside the EU you will need to make use of private treatment, which is expensive, so travel insurance to cover this is an essential precaution.

Medical Services

The Greek Red Cross has recently set up a round-the-clock medical advice service for hotels throughout the mainland and the islands. The service links hotels with a Red Cross centre in Athens, where a team of 10 doctors, selected for their knowledge of languages, work on a shift system providing free advice on medical emergencies. Where required, it will indicate the most suitable hospital for treatment of a specific emergency. The aim is to cut down on delays in providing treatment, either locally or in the nearest suitable hospital.

The European Health Advocacy also provides a range of services in a number of languages. Contact Kolofontas 3, Athens (tel: 723-4621).

Most doctors pride themselves on their English. Look for the sign IATPEION, indicating a doctor's clinic or surgery.

Dentist: Antony Alaxouzos, 40 Odos Amerikis, Rhodes Town (tel: 28459).

Minor Illnesses

You can buy across-the-counter medicines at pharmacies in the major resorts to treat any minor accident or illness, but it is worth taking a small medical kit including an analgesic, first-aid dressings and something to soothe insect bites. Minor stomach upsets should be treated with water and rehydration salts. Note that codeine is a controlled drug in Greece and you must have a prescription for it.

Mosquitoes

The very hot climate of Rhodes is, as one would expect, the kind that attracts reptiles, insects – mosquitoes included – and a variety of other animal life. These are not dangerous, although mosquitoes are often a real nuisance. It is advisable to take precautions to avoid this irritating creature from causing you any discomfort. The most effective way is by using tablets with electrical hotplates. You simply plug them in overnight in a ventilated area, away from draughts. Alternatively, coils which you leave to smoulder like incense sticks, as well as sprays, are also available; sprays are best applied just before dark, with the windows closed for a while. When out of doors you can use an insect repellent; some are in roll-on form, like deodorants.

Sunburn
Sunburn can also be a major health problem, so make sure you use a good barrier cream and go for a steady tan; remember, even when the breeze blows you can still burn.

Water
Although the water is considered quite safe to drink, most visitors prefer to avoid tap water and ice and use bottled water, which is available at all bars, restaurants, hotels and supermarkets.

Holidays
On public and religious holidays most shops close for the day; they also close the afternoon before and the morning after a religious holiday. If a national holiday falls on a Sunday it is the following Monday which is observed. Note that the Greek Orthodox Easter can fall several weeks before or after the Catholic Easter. The following are public holidays:
1 January; 6 January (Epiphany); 25 March (Independence Day); Orthodox Good Friday, Easter Sunday and Easter Monday (March/April); 1 May (Labour Day); Whit Monday (May/June); 15 August (Feast of the Assumption); 28 October (Okhi Day) – commemorating when, in 1940, Greece rejected Mussolini's ultimatum and entered the war on the side of the Allies; Christmas Day and Boxing Day.

Lost Property
For property lost in your hotel, report to the management or travel representative in the first instance, and then to the local police station. For articles lost elsewhere, contact the police on 100 or visit the police station in Rhodes Town.

Media

Newspapers
Overseas newspapers are available in Rhodes about a day after publication. They are obtainable in and around Mandraki Harbour, in Rhodes Town, and also in some of the larger hotels. For faster news in English, look out for *Athens News*, published daily except Mondays. The magazine *Where and What* gives general information in English, German and Swedish, while the English-language newspaper *Rhodes Gazette*, published from April to the end of October, is available at the tourist office. Most hotels sell newspapers and magazines, but for the biggest selection of foreign periodicals try the news-stand in the arcaded entrance to the market-place at Mandraki Harbour, or alternatively the bookstalls in front of the main post office.

Radio
Some Greek radio stations sometimes have programmes of interest to the foreign listener. ERA1, located at 1008KHz and 297.6m or 91.80MHz, presents the news in English daily at 07.30hrs, preceded by a weather

forecast and sea conditions programme at 06.30hrs. ERA2, on 981KHz and 305.8m, has two newscasts daily in English and French, going out at 14.20 and 21.20hrs. To receive the BBC World Service, tune to the 49 metres band on short wave; in the evening, try medium wave.

Television

There are nine television channels including two Greek, one Turkish, one German, one French, one English/American, and one continuous news. The channels ET 1 and 2 show numerous programmes and films in English with Greek subtitles.

Money Matters

The unit of currency is the drachma. The most common notes in circulation are those of 50,100, 500, 1,000 and 5,000 drachmas, and coins of 1 and 2 drs (bronze), 5, 10 and 20 drs (nickel) and 50 and 100 drs (gold/bronze). You are officially allowed to take just 100,000 drachmas into Rhodes with you. Upon your return, no more than 40,000 drachmas may be taken out of Greece. There are no restrictions on the import or export of foreign currency up to the equivalent of $1,000 but amounts in excess of this must be declared to the Currency Control Authorities on your arrival in Rhodes.

Traditional island costume is worn only on very special occasions

Exchange

Most visitors take their money in the form of travellers' cheques, but a small amount of local currency is worth acquiring in advance, especially if arriving at weekends when banks and some currency exchange offices will be closed. Cash, travellers' cheques and Eurocheques can be exchanged at banks and post offices and many travel and tour agencies. The rate of exchange varies from day to day, but is the same at all banks and post offices. Eurocheques must be made out in drachmas, and you pay a commissioning charge of around 1.6 per cent to the exchanging bank, plus a handling fee per transaction. Travellers' cheques are also widely accepted in shops and restaurants, but at lower exchange rates than banks. Most major credit cards are fairly widely accepted in the larger resorts, but only by the more expensive shops, hotels and restaurants. They are particularly useful for large purchases, like renting cars, but are no use in tavernas.

Banks
The major Greek banks, including the National Bank of Greece, the Commercial Bank of Greece, the Bank of Greece and the Ionian and Popular, have branches in Rhodes Town. In the Old Town are: Commercial Bank, Plateía Mouseio; Ionian and Popular Bank, Plateía Sýmis; National Bank of Greece, Plateía Mouseio. New Town: National Bank of Greece, Plateía Kiprou; Bank of Greece, Mandraki Harbour. Cash may be obtained at the National Bank for Eurocard and Visa holders,

Enjoying coffee and conversation

and at the Commercial Bank for Diners Club holders. If you lose money, contact the police and take your passport with you. The police will give you a form to forward to your insurance company.
If you travel to Turkey from Rhodes, remember that you cannot obtain Turkish currency in Greece or exchange Greek currency for Turkish when you get there. You should either arm yourself with some American dollars – which can be obtained from Greek banks – or cash one of your own travellers' cheques on arrival.

Opening Times

Shops: Those selling jewellery, cosmetics, records and cassettes, leather goods and shoes are usually open daily, including holidays, 08.00–13.00hrs and again 17.00–22.00hrs; Sundays 10.00–14.00hrs. Other shops, and dry-cleaners, open Monday to Friday 08.00–13.00hrs and again 17.00–21.00hrs; Saturdays 08.00–13.00hrs; Sundays and holidays 10.00–14.00hrs.

Banks: Monday to Friday 08.00–14.00hrs, and also Saturday mornings for the exchange of currency and/or travellers' cheques. In summer some banks open Monday to Friday 08.00–13.00hrs and 17.00–21.00hrs; Saturdays 08.00–13.00hrs.

Car Repair Workshops: Monday to Saturday 07.30–15.30hrs; closed Sundays and holidays.

Hairdressers: Women's – Monday to Friday 09.00–21.00hrs; Saturdays 09.00–20.00hrs; Sundays and holidays 09.00–12.00hrs. Men's – Monday to Friday 08.00–21.00hrs; Saturdays 09.00–19.00hrs. Closed Sundays and holidays.

Museums and Sites: Most museums and places of interest open Tuesday to Saturday 08.30–15.00hrs; Sundays and holidays 08.30–15.00hrs. Closed Mondays. All are closed on 25 December, 1 January, 25 March, Good Friday and Easter.

Nightclubs: All close at 02.30hrs at the latest.

Restaurants: Lunch 11.00–15.00hrs; dinner 18.00hrs till midnight.

Personal Safety

Watch out for the lethal three-sided lifts fitted in many hotels in Rhodes. These lifts have no inner door, so as they move, passengers run the risk of abrasion or worse against the wall. A few lifts carry signs warning children not to use the lift without an adult present, but it is advisable to take extra care. Many hotel swimming pools fail to have depth markings, so care is required here, too, especially with children.
Women travellers to Rhodes should not be troubled by sexual harassment from local males, as Greek men, particularly away from the main tourist spots, are generally respectful of women. A firm 'no' is usually enough to deter anyone making advances.

Greek Orthodox priests are traditionally bearded and their long hair is kept neatly under a black chimneypot hat

Pharmacies
Known as *Farmakia*, they can be identified by their sign of a red, green or blue cross on a white background. A rota system is in operation throughout the island, so there is always one pharmacy open at any time of day or night. You can obtain the address of the nearest duty pharmacy from your hotel desk or by contacting the Police.
Most are open from 08.30–13.30/14.30hrs Monday to Saturday, and also from 17.00–20.00hrs on Sundays. The majority of pharmacies provide the normal remedies and are happy to give advice on minor ailments. Most items are available without prescription, although medicines are not particularly cheap.

Places of Worship
Roman Catholic: at St Mary's, off Odos Kaphopoule, a mass is said in Latin on weekdays (and on Saturdays in the tourist season) at 19.00hrs and on Sundays at 08.00. 11.00 and 19.00hrs; and at St Francis's, 28 Odos Dimokratias, services are held on Sundays at 10.00 and on weekdays at 08.30hrs.
Protestant services are held at St Mary's.
Jewish: the 17th-century Sholom Synagogue, in Odos Dosiadou, is open for prayer.
Muslim: Tzamí Souleïmán, Odos Sokratous, Old Town is open for prayer.

Police
The police (called *chorofilakes*) have green uniforms and deal with civilian problems, including those of tourists. Police headquarters are near the main post office on Plateía Eleftherías, in Rhodes Town.

Post Offices
The main post offices on Rhodes can be found on Plateía Eleftherías at Mandraki Harbour in Rhodes Town, and there is another, in the Old Town, on Odos Orfeos.
Sending letters or postcards by surface mail can take a considerable time. Airmail is quicker, but even by this method letters take three to six days to reach the rest of Europe, five to eight days to reach North America, and a little longer to Australia and New Zealand. Postcards can be very slow indeed: up to two weeks for Europe, a month to North America or the Pacific. A modest fee for express service

cuts letter delivery time to about two days for the UK and three days for North America. There is a basic fee for airmail letters (the first 20 grams within Europe, the first 10 grams for North America), then a further fee for successive weight divisions (20–50 grams for Europe, 10–20 grams for North America). Parcels must be taken to a post office for inspection and wrapped afterwards, so take wrapping paper, sticky-tape, string, scissors and a pen with you.

Opening times: main branch, 08.00–20.00hrs in summer, 08.00–19.00hrs in winter; Old Town office, Monday to Friday 08.00–20.00hrs, Saturdays and Sundays 09.00–18.00hrs. Reception desks of the larger hotels normally sell postage stamps, and post boxes are yellow and black with a hunting horn design.

Public Transport

Buses

Rhodes Town is the centre of public transport, and buses from here go all over the island, which is well served by roads. Services are fairly regular and inexpensive, but buses tend to become very crowded in the high season, and are much less frequent out of season and on Sundays and holidays. Two companies – KTEL and RODA – provide the local bus services. KTEL operates along the east coast, while the west coast is RODA territory. The two lines meet only rarely. The two bus stations are within a hundred yards/metres or so of each other at the back of the New Market. The KTEL concourse is beside the Municipal Gardens; RODA departures are from Odos Averof, immediately behind the New Market. In addition, there are five city buses which run until 22.00 or 23.00hrs. Buses to the airport depart approximately every 45 minutes from the Olympic Airways premises on the left of Odos Ierou Lohou, beyond the Plaza Hotel. Tickets

Playing **tavli** *(backgammon) in a* **kafeneion**

are bought on the bus before departure; it may be worth purchasing a day pass.

Boats

The main passenger ferry port on the island is the Commercial Harbour. There are scheduled stopping services to all of the Dodecanese islands as well as to Piraeus, Crete, Italy and Turkey. The journey time depends on the number of ports of call. There is a faster hydrofoil service, known as the Flying Dolphin, which operates services in the high season to Kós, Sými and Pátmos. From Mandraki Harbour some tour companies operate small coastal vessels for day trips to other destinations along the coast, including Líndos. Caïque trips to Chálki leave from Kameíros Skála in season. Seats can be booked through the agent at 2 Odos Papagou, opposite the KTEL bus station. The bigger boats are served by the DANE agency, 95 Odos Amerikis (tel: 77070), the Kydon Agency, Etgelondon Dodekanissiou (tel: 23000) and Skevos Travel, 111 Odos Amerikas (tel: 22461).

Taxis

Taxis are privately owned, but can be booked by telephoning 27666. This is the number of the main taxi rank in Rhodes Town, in Plateía Riminí, at Mandraki Harbour. In rural areas, the type of taxi used is known as an *agoreon*. This has no meter, rates being fixed for specific distances or zones.

Senior Citizens

Many travel companies offer attractive rates to senior citizens booking an out-of-season holiday of several weeks – contact your travel agent for information. Outside the hustle and bustle of the main holiday season, when the weather is more temperate, the natural beauty of the island offers much for the older visitors to enjoy. They would be well advised to avoid the bigger, longer-established resorts, however, where noise could be troublesome.

Student and Youth Travel

Students of any age should obtain an International Student Identity Card, ensuring discounts not only in respect of travel, but also on entry to museums, archaeological sites and some forms of entertainment on Rhodes. Anyone under 26, but not a student, may consider applying for membership of the Federation of International Youth Travel Organisations, which guarantees discounts from some ferry and tour operators.

Telephones

You can make a phone call from one of the two OTE (Organismos Telephikinonion Ellathos – Greek Telecommunications Organisation) offices in Rhodes Town, or from a call box. The central office of the OTE is located at the corner of Amerikis and 25 Martiou streets. There are ten direct-dial telephones available in service seven days a week, from 06.00hrs until midnight, from April to October;

at other times the service closes at 23.00hrs. International calls are metered, and you pay the cashier after your call. Blue and red phones you see elsewhere are for local calls; orange ones for long distance. International direct dialling is prefixed by the code 00 followed by the country code (1 for the US and Canada, 44 for the UK, 61 for Australia, 64 for New Zealand and 353 for the Republic of Ireland), area code and number. An English-speaking operator can help on 162. To call Britain, for example, dial 00 44, the area code without the initial 0, and then the number. To call Rhodes from overseas, dial the international code for Greece (01030), followed by 241, for Rhodes, followed by the number you require.

Useful Numbers
Rhodes Telephone Code: 0241
English-speaking International Operator: 162
Fire Brigade: 199
National Tourist Organisation of Greece: 23255, 23655
Líndos Telephone Code: 0244
Líndos Information Office: 31428; Municipality Information Office: 35945
Olympic Airways: 24555
Port Authority: 27365
Recorded instructions for international calls: 169
Telephone information: local, 131; international, 162
Weather: 149

Time
Greek time is two hours ahead of Greenwich Mean Time and British Summer Time, except for short periods in the spring and autumn when Greek clocks are changed in advance of British clocks. Local time is seven hours ahead of US and Canada Eastern Time, and eight hours behind Australian and New Zealand Time.

A roadside ikonostasis *(shrine) often marks the scene of a fatal accident or a narrow escape*

Tipping
By law, service charges are included in the bills at hotels, tavernas and restaurants. However, a little extra is appreciated if good service has been provided. In general, 10 per cent is a satisfactory amount to leave as a tip.

Toilets
Greek plumbing leaves a lot to

be desired. The ancient Greeks may have been the pioneers of civilisation, but the new generation are certainly low on the list in the plumbing league. although, to be fair, things have improved considerably in recent years. However, with the influx of tourists, some anomalies in the plumbing systems are bound to occur throughout the season, especially during July and August. Small hotels and *pension*-type places usually request guests to place used toilet paper in a pedal bin. The reason is that the pipes are narrow, so if you fail to follow the instructions you block the lavatory. Rhodes Town has several public toilets, generally reasonably clean and well maintained. They can be found in the Neá Agorá (New Market), at Mandraki Harbour; on Odos Alexandrou Papagou, near the bus terminus; at the office of Olympic Airways, in Odos Ierou Lohou, in the New Town; and, in the Old Town, in Odos Orfeos between the Grand Masters' Palace Gates and the Clock Tower.

Tourist Offices

The National Tourist Organisation of Greece (NTOG) maintains offices in:
Australia and New Zealand: 51–57 Pitt Street, Sydney, NSW 2000 (tel: 2411 663)
Canada: 1300 Bay Street, Toronto, Ontario, M5R 3K8 (tel: 9682 220); 1233 rue de la Montagne, Montréal, Quebec, H3G 1Z2 (tel: 871 1535)
UK and Republic of Ireland: 4 Conduit Street, London W1R 0DJ (tel: 0171-734 5997)
USA: 645 Fifth Avenue, Olympic Tower, New York, NY 10022 (tel: 212-421 5777); 611 West Sixth Street, Suite 2198, Los Angeles, California 90017 (tel: 213-626 6696); 168 North Michigan Avenue, National Bank of Greece Building, Chicago, Illinois 6-601 (tel: 312-782 1084).
On Rhodes, the National Tourist Organisation of Greece provides useful, free brochures, maps, timetables and programmes of events. Its main office is found in the centre of Rhodes New Town on Odos Makariou (tel: 23655, 23255), where the staff will advise on hotels, car rental or sightseeing. The office also stocks a good supply of general information literature. Most of the staff speak English, French or German as well as Greek. The office is open from 07.30 until 15.00hrs. Tourist information desks are also operated by the municipal authorities of Rhodes at the airport, at the port, and in the Old Town. They are open daily from 07.30 until 20.00hrs. Here, too, information is provided in various languages. There is also a tourist information office in Líndos, in the main square.

Travel Agencies

There are numerous travel agencies in Rhodes Town and in all the major holiday resorts throughout the island which will arrange accommodation for you, book airline tickets, or organise sightseeing tours. Among the most respected is **Rodos Express**, in Papanikolaou and Amerikis streets, Rhodes Town (tel: 21303).

LANGUAGE

Unless you know the Greek script, a vocabulary is not of very much use to the visitor. But it is helpful to know the alphabet, so that you can find your way around; and the following few basic words and phrases will help too.

Alphabet

Alpha	Αα	short a, as in hat
Beta	Ββ	v sound
Gamma	Γγ	guttural g sound
Delta	Δδ	hard th, as in father
Epsilon	Εε	short e
Zita	Ζζ	z sound
Eta	Ηη	long e, as in feet
Theta	Θθ	soft th, as in think
Iota	Ιι	short i, as in hit
Kappa	Κκ	k sound
Lambda	Λλ	l sound
Mu	Μμ	m sound
Nu	Νν	n sound
Xi	Ξξ	x or ks sound
Omicron	Οο	short o, as in pot
Pi	Ππ	p sound
Rho	Ρρ	r sound
Sigma	Σσ	s sound
Tau	Ττ	t sound
Ipsilon	Υυ	another ee sound, or y as in funny
Phi	Φφ	f sound
Chi	Χχ	guttural ch, as in loch
Psi	Ψψ	ps, as in chops
Omega	Ωω	long o, as in bone

Numbers

1	éna	14	dekatéssera
2	dío	15	dekapénde
3	tria	16	dekaéxi
4	téssera	17	dekaeptá
5	pénde	18	dekaokto
6	éxi	19	dekaennía
7	eptá	20	ikosi
8	októ	30	triánda
9	ennía	40	saránda
10	déka	50	penínda
11	éndeka	100	ekató
12	dódeka	101	ekaton éna
13	dekatría	1000	chília

In myth the sun god's chariot drives over the horizontal sunset

Basic Vocabulary
good morning kaliméra
good evening kalispéra
goodnight kaliníkta
goodbye chérete
hello yásou
thank you efcharistó
please/you're welcome parakaló
yes ne
no óchi
where is...? poo íne?
how much is...? póso káni?
I would like tha íthela
do you speak English? milate angliká?
I don't speak Greek then miló helliniká

Places
street ódos
avenue léofóros
square plateía
restaurant estiatório
hotel xenodochío
room domátio
post office tachithromío
letter grámma
stamps grammatóssima
police astinomía
customs teloniakos
passport diavatírion
pharmacy farmakío
doctor iatrós
dentist odontiatrós
entrance ísothos
exit éxothos
bank trápeza
church eklisía
hospital nosokomío
café kafeneion

Travelling
car aftokínito
bus leoforío
train tréno
boat karávi
garage garáz
train station stathmos
bus station stasi ton leoforío
airport aerodrómio
ticket isitírio

Food and Drink
food fagitó
bread psomí
water neró
wine krasí
beer bira
coffee kafé

Fish
lobster astakós
squid kalamarákia
octopus oktapóthi
red mullet barboúnia
whitebait maríthes
sea bream sinagrítha

Meat/Poultry
lamb arnáki
chicken kotópoulo
meat on a skewer souvlákia
liver skóti

Vegetables
spinach spanáki
courgette kolokithia
beans fasólia

Salads and Starters
olives eliés
yoghurt and cucumber dip tzatsiki
tomato and cucumber salad angour domata
stuffed vine leaves dolmades
'Greek' salad with cheese horiatiki

Desserts
honeycake baklavá
honey puffs loukoumádes
semolina cake halvá
ice-cream pagotó
yoghurt yiaourti
custard tart bougatsa

INDEX

Page numbers in *italics* refer to illustrations.

Acknowledgements
The Automobile Association would like to thank the following photographers, libraries and associations for their assistance in the preparation of this book:

TIM LARSEN-COLLINGE took all the pictures in this book (© AA PHOTO LIBRARY) except:
J ALLAN CASH PHOTOLIBRARY 75 Sými.
SPECTRUM COLOUR LIBRARY 5 Silhouettes, 9 Temple of Apollo, 17 Platia Ippokratous, 107 Fishermen.
INTERNATIONAL PHOTOBANK Cover Town Harbour & windmills, 39 Líndhos, 41 Acropolis Líndhos, 43 Ormiskos Líndhos, 44 Líndhos Bay Hotel, 51 52 Falirakion Beach, 58 Ixós, 61 Hotel Rodos Palace, Ixós, 98/9 Líndos.
MARY EVANS PICTURE LIBRARY 10/11 Colossus of Rhodes.
NATURE PHOTOGRAPHERS LTD 84 Bee-eater (K J Carlson), 87 Jersey tiger moth, 89 Purple spurge (A J Cleave).

Contributors for this revision:
Verifier: Robin Gauldie; Copy editor: Hilary Hughes

The Automobile Association would also like to thank the **ELPA (Automobile and Touring Club of Greece)** for their assistance in updating the Directory section for this revised edition.